CONTE

INTERMEDIATE CHINESE SHORT STORIES

10 Captivating Short Stories to Learn Chinese & Grow Your Vocabulary the Fun Way!

Intermediate Chinese Stories

www.LingoMastery.com

INTRODUCTION

Hello, Reader!

If you've considered reading this book, then you must have made pretty impressive progress in learning Chinese. That's awesome! However, we don't want you to be one of the language learners who have to say: "I only know enough Chinese to order at a Chinese restaurant" because they stopped after the initial success. Constantly challenging yourself is the key to perfection and we encourage you to reach it no matter how good you are now.

This book is a collection of 10 Short Stories in Chinese which were specially written for Chinese intermediate and advanced learners, as we seek to provide a comprehensive experience in the language and to expose you to a rich and practical vocabulary, useful grammar structures and expressions that would allow you to take the Chinese language knowledge and skills to a new level.

Reading has been proven to be one of the most efficient ways to learn a foreign language, as it helps the student to become familiar with the proper grammar use, the rhythms, forms and rules of the language; also, according to research, it exposes the pupil to more sentences per minute than the average movie or TV show.

When creating this book, we were balancing between making it both entertaining and challenging. If you feel it's time to read this book, then you must have gone far along the way of mastering Chinees. The knowledge and vocabulary you already have will allow you to enjoy reading. Yet the book presents new sentence structures, grammatical richness and varying usage of the language, motivating you to explore further along the journey of learning Chinese.

The stories cover a variety of topics, from Chinese history and culture to the life in today's China, in formal narrartive form and casual dialogues representing the actual everyday conversations. This will prepare our language learners with a better understanding of the context so that they can use Chinese more confidently. Additionally, at the end of each story, a learning support section will help you whenever you need it by providing you with English translations of difficult words, a summary of the story and multiple-choice questions about important features of the story. This will allow you to follow all the details of each story and, thus, to improve at a fast pace.

We have carefully created this book to make it helpful, interesting, and inspoiring, while considering what you, as a reader, already have and will need. We hope that you find this book genuinely entertaining for both academic and casual reading.

FREE BOOK!

Free Book Reveals The 6 Step Blueprint That Took Students
From Language Learners To Fluent In 3 Months

One last thing before we start. If you haven't already, head over to
LingoMastery.com/hacks and grab a copy of our free Lingo Hacks
book that will teach you the important secrets that you need to know
to become fluent in a language as fast as possible. Again, you can find
the free book over at **LingoMastery.com/hacks**.

Now, without further ado, enjoy these Chinese Stories for
Intermediate learners.

Good luck, reader!

Chapter 1

中秋节 (ZHŌNG QIŪ JIÉ)

每年的**农历**八月十五是中国的一个重要**传统节日**，**中秋节**，大约是**公历**的九月到十月初。因为按照中国的农历，八月是秋季的第二个月，因此八月十五在古代**民间**就被称为中秋，意思是秋季的中间点。

měi nián de **nóng lì** bā yuè shí wǔ shì zhōng guó de yī gè zhòng yào **chuán tǒng jié rì**, **zhōng qiū jié**, dà yuē shì **gōng lì** de jiǔ yuè dào shí yuè chū. yīn wéi àn zhào zhōng guó de nóng lì, bā yuè shì qiū jì de dì èr gè yuè, yīn cǐ bā yuè shí wǔ zài gǔ dài **mín jiān** jiù bèi chēng wéi zhōng qiū, yì sī shì qiū jì de zhōng jiān diǎn.

中秋节始于中国古代的**唐朝**，有全家人**团圆**赏月的**习俗**。同时，中秋节也是秋季**农作物**收获的时节，因此人们在中秋**祭**月，也有**庆祝丰收**，感谢神明的意义。

zhōng qiū jié shǐ yú zhōng guó gǔ dài de **táng cháo**, yǒu quán jiā rén **tuán yuán** shǎng yuè de **xí sú**. tóng shí, zhōng qiū jié yě shì qiū jì **nóng zuò wù** shōu huò de shí jié, yīn cǐ rén men zài zhōng qiū **jì** yuè, yě yǒu **qìng zhù fēng shōu**, gǎnxiè shénmíng de yìyì.

关于中秋节，有一个美丽的传说。**远古**的时候，天上有十个太阳，令河海干枯，大地**寸草不生**，人民苦不堪言。有个叫后羿的英雄，力大无比又十分**英勇**，为了**解救**百姓，他**射**下了九个

4

太阳，留下一个继续为天地发光发热。从此后羿深受人们的尊敬和**爱戴**，并从神仙西王母那里得到了一包不死药，吃了可以**长生不老**，升天成仙。

guān yú zhōng qiū jié, yǒu yī gè měi lì de chuán shuō. **yuǎn gǔ** de shí hòu, tiān shàng yǒu shí gè tài yáng, lìng hé hǎi gàn kū, dà dì **cùn cǎo bù shēng**, rén mín **kǔ bú kān yán**. yǒu gè jiào hòu yì de yīng xióng, lì dà wú bǐ yòu shí fèn **yīng yǒng**, wéi le **jiě jiù** bǎi xìng, tā **shè** xià le jiǔ gè tài yáng, liú xià yī gè jì xù wéi tiān dì fā guāng fā rè. cóng cǐ hòu yì shēn shòu rén men de zūn jìng hé **ài dài**, bìng cóng shén xiān xī wáng mǔ nà lǐ dé dào le yī bāo bú sǐ yào, chī le kě yǐ **cháng shēng bú lǎo**, shēng tiān chéng **xiān**.

后羿的妻子名叫嫦娥，美丽**贤慧**，心地**善良**。后羿便把不死药交给嫦娥保管。后羿有一个徒弟名叫逢蒙，是位**奸诈**小人。他也想长生不老，于是就在这一年的八月十五，趁着后羿出门**打猎**，**闯进**后羿家里，**逼迫**嫦娥交出不死药。嫦娥无力反抗，**仓促**之间只好把药全都吞下。

hòu yì de qī zǐ míng jiào cháng é, měi lì **xián huì**, xīn dì **shàn liáng**. hòu yì biàn bǎ bú sǐ yào jiāo gěi cháng é bǎo guǎn. hòu yì yǒu yī gè tú dì míng jiào féng méng, shì wèi **jiān zhà** xiǎo rén. tā yě xiǎng zhǎng shēng bú lǎ, yú shì jiù zài zhè yī nián de bā yuè shí wǔ, chèn zhe hòu yì chū mén **dǎ liè**, **chuǎng jìn** hòu yì jiā lǐ, **bī pò** cháng é jiāo chū bú sǐ yào. cháng é wú lì fǎn kàng, **cāng cù** zhī jiān zhī hǎo bǎ yào quán dōu tūn xià.

马上，她便**身轻如燕**，飘出窗口飞上天空。由于嫦娥舍不得离开自己的丈夫，就在离**地球**最近的月亮上停了下来，留在月亮上的广寒宫。

mǎ shàng, tā biàn **shēn qīng rú yàn**, piāo chū chuāng kǒu fēi shàng tiān kōng. yóu yú cháng é shě bú dé lí kāi zì jǐ de zhàng fū, jiù zài lí dì qiú zuì jìn de yuè liàng shàng tíng le xià lái, liú zài yuè liàng shàng de guǎng hán gōng.

听到消息，后羿十分**痛苦**，望着夜空**思念妻子**。他惊奇地发现**皎洁**明亮的月亮中似乎有人的身影，就像是嫦娥。于是此后每年的八月十五，他都会在月光下准备嫦娥喜爱的糕点水果，思念嫦娥。而嫦娥也会走出月宫，遥望地球，思念**丈夫**和乡亲们。从此**代代相传**，变成了中秋节。

tīng dào xiāo xī, hòu yì shí fèn **tòng kǔ**, wàng zhe yè kōng **sī niàn qī zǐ**. tā jīng qí dì fā xiàn **jiǎo jié** míng liàng de yuè liàng zhōng sì hū yǒu rén de shēn yǐng, jiù xiàng shì cháng é. yú shì cǐ hòu měi nián de bā yuè shí wǔ, tā dōu huì zài yuè guāng xià zhǔn bèi cháng é xǐ ài de gāo diǎn shuǐ guǒ, sī niàn cháng é. ér cháng é yě huì zǒu chū yuè gōng, yáo wàng dì qiú, sī niàn **zhàng fū** hé xiāng qīn men. cóng cǐ **dài dài xiàng chuán**, biàn chéng le zhōng qiū jié.

如今的中秋节是一个全国性**假期**，也是中国人心中一家人一起庆祝的重要节日。中秋节最重要的食品是**月饼**，圆形的月饼也象征着圆满和团圆。**饼皮**用**面粉**烤制而成，传统的**馅**有**豆沙**、**百果**、**五仁**、**鲜肉**、**蛋黄**等等。还有许多现代新口味，包括**巧克力**、**椰蓉**、**菠萝**等等。还有这个季节的时令新鲜水果，比如**柚子**、**栗子**、**柿子**等等。中秋节这一天晚上是**满月**，只要天气好，就能看见圆圆的月亮，银色的月光照亮了大地。抬头看着月亮，不知道嫦娥是否还在那里呢？

rú jīn de zhōng qiū jié shì yī gè quán guó xìng **jià qī**, yě shì zhōng guó rén xīn zhōng yī jiā rén yī qǐ qìng zhù de zhòng yào jié rì. zhōng qiū jié zuì zhòng yào de shí pǐn shì **yuè bǐng**, yuán xíng de yuè bǐng yě xiàng zhēng zhe yuán mǎn hé tuán yuán. **bǐng pí** yòng **miàn fěn** kǎo zhì ér chéng, chuán tǒng de **xiàn** yǒu **dòu shā, bǎi guǒ, wǔ rén,**

xiān ròu, dàn huáng děng děng. hái yǒu xǔ duō xiàn dài xīn kǒu wèi, bāo kuò **qiǎo kè lì, yē róng, bō luó** děng děng. hái yǒu zhè gè jì jié de shí lìng xīn xiān shuǐ guǒ, bǐ rú **yòu zǐ, lì zǐ, shì zǐ** děng děng. zhōng qiū jié zhè yī tiān wǎn shàng shì **mǎn yuè**, zhī yào tiān qì hǎo, jiù néng kàn jiàn yuán yuán de yuè liàng, yín sè de yuè guāng zhào liàng le dà dì. tái tóu kàn zhe yuè liàng, bú zhī dào cháng é shì fǒu hái zài nà lǐ ne?

即使不能在一起度过这个节日，人们也会和亲人互通电话或者通过**网络**聊天。中国古代诗人张九龄，曾经在诗中写道：海上生明月，天涯共此时。意思是：一轮皎洁的明月从海上**徐徐**升起，我望着月亮的同时，在遥远的地方，你也在望着月亮，虽然我们不在一起，但也能共享同一轮明月。这种通过月亮来寄托思念和牵挂的方式，就是中国人对中秋节的感情。

jí shǐ bú néng zài yī qǐ dù guò zhè gè jié rì, rén men yě huì hé qīn rén hù tōng diàn huà huò zhě tōng guò **wǎng luò** liáo tiān. zhōng guó gǔ dài shī rén zhāng jiǔ líng céng jīng zài shī zhōng xiě dào: hǎi shàng shēng míng yuè, tiān yá gòng cǐ shí. yì sī shì: yī lún jiǎo jié de míng yuè cóng hǎi shàng **xú xú** shēng qǐ, wǒ wàng zhe yuè liàng de tóng shí, zài yáo yuǎn de dì fāng, nǐ yě zài wàng zhe yuè liàng, suī rán wǒ men bú zài yī qǐ, dàn yě néng gòng xiǎng tóng yī lún míng yuè. zhè zhǒng tōng guò yuè liàng lái jì tuō sī niàn hé qiān guà de fāng shì, jiù shì zhōng guó rén duì zhōng qiū jié de gǎn qíng.

总结 (zǒng jié- Summary

中秋节是中国的传统节日，具有悠久的历史和文化内涵。它的背后有一个凄美的神话传说。中秋节在中国人心中具有很重要的地位，因为它象征着家庭团圆。

zhōng qiū jié shì zhōng guó de chuán tǒng jié rì, jù yǒu yōu jiǔ de lì shǐ hé wén huà nèi hán. tā de bèi hòu yǒu yī gè qīměi de shén huà chuán shuō. zhōng qiū jié zài zhōng guó rén xīn zhōng jù yǒu hěn zhòng yào de dì wèi, yīn wéi tā xiàng zhēng zhe jiā tíng tuán yuán.

Summary of the story

With its long-lasting history and rich culture, the Mid-Autumn Festival is a traditional festival celebrated in China. It's associated with a beautiful legend story, although with a regretful ending. The Mid-Autumn Festival holds an important position for the Chinese people because it is a symbol of family reunion.

Vocabulary

- 农历 (nóng lì): Lunar calendar
- 传统 (chuán tǒng): traditional
- 节日 (jié rì): festival
- 中秋节 (zhōng qiū jié): Mid-Autumn Festival
- 公历 (gōng lì): Gregorian calendar
- 民间 (mín jiān): among the ordinary people, non-governmental
- 唐朝 (táng cháo): Tang Dynasty
- 团圆 (tuán yuán): get-together, reunion
- 习俗 (xí sú): custom
- 农作物 (nóng zuò wù): agricultural produce
- 祭 (jì): worship
- 庆祝 (qìng zhù): celebrate
- 丰收 (fēng shōu): harvest
- 远古 (yuǎn gǔ): in the ancient times
- 寸草不生 (cùn cǎo bù shēng): completely barren
- 苦不堪言 (kǔ bú kān yán): to suffer unspeakable misery
- 英勇 (yīng yǒng): heroic, valiant
- 解救 (jiě jiù): rescue
- 射 (shè): shoot
- 爱戴 (ài dài): beloved
- 长生不老 (cháng shēng bú lǎo): immortal, ever-young
- 仙 (xiān): god, celestial being
- 贤惠 (xián huì): virtuous
- 善良 (shàn liáng): kind-hearted
- 奸诈 (jiān zhà): treacherous
- 打猎 (dǎ liè): to go hunting
- 闯进 (chuǎng jìn): break into

- 逼迫 **(bī pò):** force
- 仓促 **(cāng cù):** in a rush
- 身轻如燕 **(shēn qīng rú yàn):** to feel weightless, be as light and agile as a swallow
- 地球 **(dì qiú):** Earth
- 痛苦 **(tòng kǔ):** painful, painfully
- 思念 **(sī niàn):** to miss
- 妻子 **(qī zǐ):** wife
- 皎洁 **(jiǎo jié):** bright and clear
- 丈夫 **(zhàng fū):** husband
- 代代相传 **(dài dài xiàng chuán):** pass down from generation to generation
- 假期 **(jià qī):** holiday
- 月饼 **(yuè bǐng):** mooncake
- 饼皮 **(bǐng pí):** pastry crust
- 面粉 **(miàn fěn):** flour
- 馅 **(xiàn):** pastry filling
- 豆沙 **(dòu shā):** red bean paste
- 百果 **(bǎi guǒ):** various dried fruits and nuts, similar to mincemeat
- 五仁 **(wǔ rén):** five nuts
- 鲜肉 **(xiān ròu):** fresh meat
- 蛋黄 **(dàn huáng):** egg yolk
- 巧克力 **(qiǎo kè lì):** chocolate
- 椰蓉 **(yē róng):** coconut flakes, shredded coconut
- 菠萝 **(bō luó):** pineapple
- 柚子 **(yòu zǐ):** pomelo
- 栗子 **(lì zǐ):** chestnut
- 柿子 **(shì zǐ):** persimmon
- 满月 **(mǎn yuè):** full moon
- 网络 **(wǎng luò):** the Internet
- 徐徐 **(xú xú):** slowly, gently

Questions about the story

1. 中秋节是每年的哪一天？

   zhōng qiū jié shì měi nián de nǎ yī tiān?

   a) 公历八月十五

      gong lì bā yuè shí wǔ

   b) 农历八月十五

      nóng lì bā yuè shí wǔ

   c) 农历九月十五

      nóng lì jiǔ yuè shí wǔ

2. 中秋节始于中国古代的哪一个朝代？

   zhōngqiū jié shǐ yú zhōng guó gǔ dài de nǎ yī gè cháo dài?

   a) 唐朝

      táng cháo

   b) 宋朝

      song cháo

   c) 清朝

      qīng cháo

3. 在中秋节的传说里，谁吃了长生不老药？

   zài zhōng qiū jié de chuán shuō lǐ, shéi chī le cháng shēng bù lǎo yào?

   a) 后羿

      hòu yì

11

b) 嫦娥

cháng'é

c) 逢蒙

féng méng

4. 如今人们在中秋节不会做的事情是什么？

rú jīn rén men zài zhōng qiū jié bù huì zuò de shì qíng shì shén

me?

a) 一家人赏月

yī jiā rén shǎng yuè

b) 吃月饼

chī yuè bǐng

c) 上班

shàng bān

5. 中秋节在中国人心中为什么很重要？

zhōng qiū jié zài zhōng guó rén xīn zhōng wèi shé me hěn

zhòng yào?

a) 因为中国人喜欢嫦娥

yīn wéi zhōng guó rén xǐ huān cháng'é

b) 因为中国人喜欢月亮

yīn wéi zhōng guó rén xǐ huān yuè liàng

c) 因为中秋节是家庭团聚的象征

yīn wéi zhōng qiū jié shì jiā tíng tuán jù de xiàng zhēng

Answers

1. B
2. A
3. B
4. C
5. C

Chapter II

微信是什么
(WĒI XÌN SHÌ SHÉN ME)

如果你有来自中国的朋友，问问他们的**手机**上，有没有**安装**"微信"。而我敢**打赌**，答案是"有"。如果你问一个中国人，平时和人最常用的**联系方式**是什么，回答很有可能是"微信"。和中国朋友一起**游玩**的时候，如果他们用手机**拍照**，之后常常会发给"**朋友圈**"。在中国买东西的时候，不管是大**超市**还是小**摊位**，都能看到**顾客**用"微信**支付**"。

rú guǒ nǐ yǒu lái zì zhōng guó de péng yǒu, wèn wèn tā men de **shǒu jī** shàng yǒu méi yǒu **ān zhuāng** "wēi xìn". er wǒ gǎn **dǎ dǔ**, dá àn shì "yǒu". rú guǒ nǐ wèn yī gè zhōng guó rén, píng shí hé rén zuì cháng yòng de **lián xì fāng shì** shì shí me, huí dá hěn yǒu kě néng shì "wēi xìn". hé zhōng guó péng yǒu yī qǐ **yóu wán** de shí hòu, rú guǒ tā men yòng shǒu jī **pāi zhào**, zhī hòu cháng cháng huì fā gèi "**péng yǒu quān**". zài zhōng guó mǎi dōng xī de shí hòu, bú guǎn shì dà **chāo shì** hái shì xiǎo **tān wèi**, dōu néng kàn dào **gù kè** yòng "wēi xìn **zhī fù**".

到2019年第一**季度**为止，有超过11亿人是微信的**活跃用户**。在中国**几乎**无人不知，拥有**智能手机**的人几乎没有人不使用微信，包括很多在中国生活的**外国人**。它也被带到了中国以外的**世界**

各地。那么微信到底是什么呢？

dào 2019 nián dì yī **jì dù** wéi zhǐ, yǒu chāo guò 11 yì rén shì wēi xìn de **huó yuè yòng hù**. zài zhōng guó **jī hū** wú rén bùzhī, yōng yǒu **zhì néng shǒu jī** de rén jī hū méi yǒu rén bú shǐ yòng wēi xìn, bāo kuò hěn duō zài zhōng guó shēng huó de **wài guó rén**. tā yě bèi dài dào le zhōng guó yǐ wài de **shì jiè gè dì**. nà me wēi xìn dào dǐ shì shí me ne?

它是一种安装在智能手机上的**应用程序**，由腾讯公司开发，虽然2011年才**问世**，但已经在十年不到的时间里，成了无数人生活中**不可缺少**的东西。它具有像 Skype 和 Whatsapp 一样的**即时通讯**功能，包括**语音**和**视频**通话；它还有 Facebook 和 Twitter 一样的社交内容**发布**、**分享**、**评论**和**关注**功能；你也可以用它来**注册"公众号"**并发布文字、图片和视频内容，就像是**博客**；更特别的是，它还能连接到**银行账户**或**信用卡**，实现好友之间的**现金转账**和消费时的支付与收款。除了这些主要功能，微信也是一个小程序**开发平台**，可以**玩游戏**、**阅读**和做许多有趣的事情。

tā shì yī zhǒng ān zhuāng zài zhì néng shǒu jī shàng de **yīng yòng chéng xù**, yóu téng xùn gōng sī kāi fā, suī rán 2011nián cái **wèn shì**, dàn yǐ jīng zài shí nián bú dào de shí jiān lǐ chéng le wú shù rén shēng huó zhōng **bú kě quē shǎo** de dōng xī. tā jù yǒu xiàng Skype hé Whatsapp yī yàng de **jì shí tōng xùn** gōng néng, bāo kuò **yǔ yīn** hé **shì pín** tōng huà: tā hái yǒu Facebook hé Twitter yī yàng de **shè jiāo** nèi róng **fā bù**, **fèn xiǎng**, **píng lùn** hé **guān zhù** gōng néng ; nǐ yě kě yǐ yòng tā lái **zhù cè "gōng zhòng hào"** bìng fā bù wén zì, tú piàn hé shì pín nèi róng, jiù xiàng shì **bó kè:** gèng tè bié de shì, tā hái néng lián jiē dào **yín háng zhàng hù** huò **xìn yòng kǎ**, shí xiàn hǎo yǒu zhī jiān de **xiàn jīn zhuǎn zhàng** hé xiāo fèi shí de zhī fù yǔ shōu kuǎn. chú le zhè xiē zhǔ yào gōng néng, wēi xìn yě shì yī gè xiǎo chéng xù **kāi fā píng tái**, kě yǐ **wán yóu xì**, **yuè dú** hé zuò xǔ duō yǒu qù de shì qíng.

微信大大改变了中国人的生活。在它出现之前，人们用手机**发短信**和**打电话**还相当普遍，但现在几乎所有的即时通讯都使用微信。在国外生活的中国人和国内的家人朋友联系，再也不用花**高昂**的电话费了，而且只要有**网络**，就能**随时随地**视频通话。

wēi xìn dà dà gǎi biàn le zhōng guó rén de shēng huó. zài tā chū xiàn zhī qián, rén men yòng shǒu jī **fā duǎn xìn** hé **dǎ diàn huà** hái xiàng dāng pǔ biàn, dàn xiàn zài jǐ hū suǒ yǒu de jí shí tōng xùn dōu shǐ yòng wēi xìn. zài guó wài shēng huó de zhōng guó rén hé guó nèi de jiā rén péng yǒu lián xì, zài yě bú yòng huā **gāo áng** de diàn huà fèi le, ér qiě zhī yào yǒu **wǎng luò**, jiù néng **suí shí suí dì** shì pín tōng huà.

有了微信，人们出门不用再带**钱包**，只需要带手机就能购物消费。从早饭在路边买一杯**豆浆**到在**西餐厅**里吃**牛排**，从在**便利店**里买杯**咖啡**到看**电影**，从坐**地铁**到**理发**，有越来越多的地方支持微信支付。就连中国春节期间拜年发红包的传统，如今也普遍通过微信来实现了。微信甚至还提供多人**聚餐**时**分摊账单**的功能。

yǒu le wēi xìn, rén men chū mén bú yòng zài dài **qián bāo**, zhī xū yào dài shǒu jī jiù néng gòu wù xiāo fèi. cóng zǎo fàn zài lù biān mǎi yī bēi **dòu jiāng** dào zài **xī cān tīng** lǐ chī **niú pái**, cóng zài **biàn lì diàn** lǐ mǎi bēi **kā fēi** dào kàn **diàn yǐng**, cóng zuò **dì tiě** dào **lǐ fā**, yǒu yuè lái yuè duō de dì fāng zhī chí wēi xìn zhī fù. jiù lián zhōng guó chūn jiē qī jiān bài nián fā hóng bāo de chuán tǒng, rú jīn yě pǔ biàn tōng guò wēi xìn lái shí xiàn le. wēi xìn shèn zhì hái tí gòng duō rén **jù cān** shí **fēn tān zhàng dān** de gōng néng.

微信的"朋友圈"更是相识的人们分享和了解**彼此**情况的重要方式。它就像是中国的 Facebook 或 Twitter，让你发布自己的照片和文字，同时看到微信联系人发布的内容，也可以**留言**评论，或表示支持和喜欢。

wēi xìn de "péng yǒu quān"gèng shì xiàng shí de rén men fèn xiǎng hé liǎo jiě **bǐ cǐ** qíng kuàng de zhòng yào fāng shì. tā jiù xiàng shì zhōng guó de Facebook huò Twitter, ràng nǐ fā bù zì jǐ de zhào piàn hé wén zì, tóng shí kàn dào wēi xìn lián xì rén fā bù de nèi róng, yě kě yǐ **liú yán** píng lùn, huò biǎo shì zhī chí hé xǐ huān.

朋友圈里的内容只有联系人才能看到，此外，微信还有一项"公众号"功能。个人或者组织都可以注册公众号，面对**公众**发布内容，就像**报纸**。用户也可以像**订阅**报纸一样订阅公众号，目前是**免费**的，这样就可以及时看到内容的**更新**。通过微信把公众号里的内容**转发**给好友，或者分享到朋友圈也都非常方便。公众号的内容**无所不有**，像是**新闻、娱乐、旅游、美食、科技、教育**……等，每一个人都能找到满足自己兴趣的公众号。

péng yǒu quān lǐ de nèi róng zhī yǒu lián xì rén cái néng kàn dào, cǐ wài, wēi xìn hái yǒu yī xiàng "gōng zhòng hào" gōng néng. gè rén huò zhě zǔ zhī dōu kě yǐ zhù cè gōng zhòng hào, miàn duì **gōng zhòng** fā bù nèi róng, jiù xiàng **bào zhǐ**. yòng hù yě kě yǐ xiàng **dìng yuè** bào zhǐ yī yàng dìng yuè gōng zhòng hào, mù qián shì **miǎn fèi** de, zhè yàng jiù kě yǐ jí shí kàn dào nèi róng de **gēng xīn**. tōng guò wēi xìn bǎ gōng zhòng hào lǐ de nèi róng zhuǎn fā gěi hǎo yǒu, huò zhě fèn xiǎng dào péng yǒu quān yě dōu fēi cháng fāng biàn. gōng zhòng hào de nèi róng wú suǒ bú yǒu, xiàng shì **xīn wén, yú lè, lǚ yóu, měi shí, kē jì, jiào yù** ……děng. měi yī gè rén dōu néng zhǎo dào mǎn zú zì jǐ xìng qù de gōng zhòng hào.

如果你想要真正融入中国，就在手机上安装微信吧！

rú guǒ nǐ xiǎng yào zhēn zhèng **róng rù** zhōng guó, jiù zài shǒu jī
shàng ān zhuāng wēi xìn ba!

总结 （zǒng jié- Summary

在中国，微信在很大程度上影响着人们的生活。它不仅仅是一个通讯和社交工具，还为人们提供娱乐、资讯、购物等功能。微信能让你真正了解**当代**中国。

zài zhōng guó, wēi xìn zài hěn dà chéng dù shàng yǐng xiǎng zhe rén men de shēng huó. tā bú jǐn jǐn shì yī gè tōng xùn hé shè jiāo gōng jù, hái wéi rén men tí gòng yú lè, zī xùn, gòu wù děng gōng néng. wēi xìn néng ràng nǐ zhēn zhèng liǎo jiě **dāng dài** zhōng guó.

Summary of the story

In China, the mobile application WeChat has a significant influence on people's life. Far more than just a tool for communications and social interactions, WeChat also provides entertainment, information feeds and purchasing functions, among others. WeChat helps you to really understand the contemporary China.

Vocabulary

- **手机 (shǒu jī)**: mobile phone
- **安装 (ān zhuāng)**: install
- **微信 (wēi xìn)**: WeChat
- **打赌 (dǎ dǔ)**: bet
- **联系方式 (lián xì fāng shì)**: contact methods
- **游玩 (yóu wán)**: tour, visit (for sight-seeing)
- **拍照 (pāi zhào)**: take a photo
- **朋友圈 (péng yǒu quān)**: circle of friends
- **超市 (chāo shì)**: supermarket
- **摊位 (tān wèi)**: street stand
- **顾客 (gù kè)**: customer, client
- **支付 (zhī fù)**: to pay, payment
- **季度 (jì dù)**: quarter (of a year)
- **活跃 (huó yuè)**: active

- **用户 (yòng hù)**: user
- **几乎 (jī hū)**: almost, nearly
- **智能手机 (zhì néng shǒu jī)**: smart phone
- **外国人 (wài guó rén)**: foreigner
- **世界各地 (shì jiè gè dì)**: all over the world
- **应用程序 (yīng yòng chéng xù)**: application (software programme)
- **问世 (wèn shì)**: appear, be lauched, be introduced
- **不可缺少 (bú kě quē shǎo)**: indispensable
- **即时通讯 (jì shí tōng xùn)**: instant communications
- **语音 (yǔ yīn)**: voice
- **视频 (shì pín)**: video
- **社交 (shè jiāo)**: social
- **发布 (fā bù)**: publish, release
- **分享 (fèn xiǎng)**: share
- **评论 (píng lùn)**: comment

- 关注 (guān zhù): follow
- 注册 (zhù cè): register
- 公众号 (gōng zhòng hào): public account
- 博客 (bó kè): blog
- 银行账户 (yín háng zhàng hù): bank account
- 信用卡 (xìn yòng kǎ): credit card
- 现金 (xiàn jīn): cash
- 转账 (zhuǎn zhàng): transaction, transfer of funds
- 开发 (kāi fā): development, to develop
- 平台 (píng tái): platform
- 玩游戏 (wán yóu xì): play games
- 阅读 (yuè dú): reading, to read books
- 发短信 (fā duǎn xìn): send a text message
- 打电话 (dǎ diàn huà): make a phone call
- 高昂 (gāo áng): expensive
- 随时随地 (suí shí suí dì): any time, anywhere
- 网络 (wǎng luò): the Internet
- 钱包 (qián bāo): wallet, purse
- 豆浆 (dòu jiāng): soy milk
- 西餐厅 (xī cān tīng): a restaurant of Western cuisine
- 牛排 (niú pái): beef steak
- 便利店 (biàn lì diàn): convenience store
- 咖啡 (kā fēi): coffee
- 电影 (diàn yǐng): movie
- 地铁 (dì tiě): underground tube, metro
- 理发 (lǐ fā): haircut
- 聚餐 (jù cān): group meal
- 分摊 (fēn tān): split up, share
- 账单 (zhàng dān): bill
- 彼此 (bǐ cǐ): each other
- 留言 (liú yán): leave a message
- 公众 (gōng zhòng): public

- 报纸 (bào zhǐ): newspaper
- 订阅 (dìng yuè): subscribe
- 免费 (miǎn fèi): for free
- 更新 (gēng xīn): update
- 新闻 (xīn wén): news
- 娱乐 (yú lè): entertainment
- 旅游 (lǚ yóu): travelling
- 美食 (měi shí): gourmet foods
- 科技 (kē jì): science and technology
- 教育 (jiào yù): education
- 融入 (róng rù): blend in
- 当代 (dāng dài): contemporary

Questions about the story

1. 微信是什么？

   wēi xìn shì shén me?

   a) 一种电脑游戏

   yī zhǒng diàn nǎo yóu xì

   b) 一种应用程序

   yī zhǒng yìng yòng chéng xù

   c) 一个网页游戏

   yī gè wǎng yè yóu xì

2. 以下哪个不是文中提到的微信功能？

   yǐ xià nǎ ge bù shì wén zhōng tí dào de wéi xìn gong néng?

   a) 聊天

   liáo tiān

   b) 支付

   zhī fù

   c) 打印

   dǎ yìn

3. 下面关于微信的说法，哪一个是正确的？

   xià miàn guān yú wēi xìn de shuō fǎ, nǎ yī gè shì zhèng què de?

   a) 只有在中国才能使用微信

   zhǐ yǒu zài zhōng guó cái néng shǐ yòng wēi xìn

   b) 只有中国人才能使用微信

   zhǐ yǒu zhòng guó rén cái néng shǐ yòng wēi xìn

23

c) 在中国以外也可以使用微信

zài zhōng guó yǐ wài yě kě yǐ shǐ yòng wēi xìn

4. 微信公众号可以发布的内容不包括？

wēi xìn gong zhòng hào kě yǐ fā bù de nèi róng bù bāo kuò?

a) 文字

wén zì

b) 图片

tú piàn

c) 盗版音乐

dào bǎn yīn yuè

5. 下面关于微信的说法哪个是不正确的？

xià miàn guān yú wēi xìn de shuō fǎ nǎ gè shì bù zhèng què de?

a) 微信让生活更加方便

wēi xìn ràng sheng huó gèng jiā fang biàn

b) 订阅微信公众号必须付费

ding yuè wēi xìn gong zhòng hào bì xū fù fèi

c) 人们喜欢通过朋友圈分享生活

rén men xǐ huān tōng guò péng yǒu quān fēn xiǎng
sheng huó

Answers

1. B
2. C
3. C
4. C
5. B

Chapter III

马可 波罗游记
(MǍ KĚ BŌ LUÓ DE YÓU JÌ)

中国和**意大利**各自拥有**悠久**的**历史**和**深厚**的文化。中国**代表**了最有**影响力**的东方文明，而意大利则**传承**了**古罗马**的**辉煌遗产**。这两个国家今天关系**友好**，文化交流**频繁**，每年都有很多中国人去意大利**旅游**，意大利人到中国游玩的也不少。不过你知道吗，在700年前就曾经有一位意大利人来到中国旅游，还写了一本著名的**游记**，他就是**马可·波罗**。

zhōng guó hé **yì dà lì** gè zì yōng yǒu **yōu jiǔ** de **lì shǐ** hé **shēn hòu** de **wén huà**. zhōng guó **dài biǎo** le zuì yǒu **yǐng xiǎng lì** de **dōng fāng wén míng**, ér yì dà lì zé **chuán chéng** le **gǔ luó mǎ** de **huī huáng yí chǎn**. zhè liǎng gè guó jiā jīn tiān guān xì **yǒu hǎo**,wén huà jiāo liú **pín fán**,měi nián dōu yǒu hěn duō zhōng guó rén qù yì dà lì **lǚ yóu**,yì dà lì rén dào zhōng guó yóu wán de yě bù shǎo. bú guò nǐ zhī dào ma,zài 700 nián qián jiù céng jīng yǒu yī wèi yì dà lì rén lái dào zhōng guó lǚ yóu,hái xiě le yī běn zhù míng de **yóu jì**,tā jiù shì **mǎ kě•bō luó**.

马可·波罗出生在十三世纪中期的**威尼斯**，当时的威尼斯**商业兴盛**，他的父亲和叔叔都因为在**远东做生意**而去到中国。当时的中国是由**蒙古统治者**建立的**元朝**，他们见到了元朝的**皇帝忽必**

烈，并把忽必烈给罗马**教皇**的信带到罗马。随后，教皇派他们俩带着回信返回中国，马可·波罗也一起去。他们在1275年到了中国，马可·波罗很受忽必烈的喜欢，并且在元朝**担任官职**。他们一家人在中国生活了近二十年后才回到**欧洲**。

mǎ kě •bō luó chū shēng zài shí sān shì jì zhōng qī de **wēi ní sī**,dāng shí de wēi ní sī **shāng yè xīng shèng**,tā de fù qīn hé shū shū dōu yīnwèi zài **yuǎn dōng zuò shēng yì** ér qù dào zhōng guó. dāng shí de zhōng guó shì yóu **méng gǔ tǒng zhì zhě** jiàn lì de **yuán cháo**,tā men jiàn dào le yuán cháo de **huáng dì hū bì liè**,bìng bǎ hū bì liè gěi luó mǎ **jiào huáng** de xìn dài dào luó mǎ. suí hòu, jiào huáng pài tā men liǎng dài zhe huí xìn fǎn huí zhōng guó,mǎ kě •bō luó yě yī qǐ qù. tā men zài 1275 nián dào le zhōng guó,mǎ kě •bō luó hěn shòu hū bì liè de xǐ huān,bìng qiě zài yuán cháo **dān rèn guān zhí**. tā men yī jiā rén zài zhōng guó shēng huó le jìn èr shí nián hòu cái huí dào **ōu zhōu**.

回到威尼斯以后，马可·波罗因为**战争**被**俘虏**，在**监狱**里把自己在中国的**经历**讲给其他人听，被记录下来，写成了《马可·波罗游记》。书中**描述**了马可·波罗在前往中国一路上的**见闻**，当时中国的社会和人们的生活情况，还**介绍**了中国周围的其他国家。当时欧洲人对东方的了解很**有限**，中国对他们来说充满了**神秘**，书中描写的内容令他们**惊奇**又**激动**，因此这本书在当时的欧洲非常**流行**。

huí dào wēi ní sī yǐ hòu,mǎ kě •bō luó yīn wéi **zhàn zhēng** bèi **fú lǔ**,zài **jiān yù** lǐ bǎ zì jǐ zài zhōng guó de **jīng lì** jiǎng gěi qí tā rén tīng,bèi jì lù xià lái,xiě chéng le <mǎ kě •bō luó yóu jì>. shū zhōng **miáo shù** le mǎ kě •bō luó zài qián wǎng zhōng guó yī lù shàng de **jiàn wén**,dāng shí zhōng guó de shè huì hé rén men de shēng huó qíng kuàng,hái **jiè shào** le zhōng guó zhōu wéi de qí tā guó jiā.

dāng shí ōu zhōu rén dùi dōng fāng de lǐao jiě hěn **yǒu xiàn,**zhōng
guó dùi tā men lái shuō chōng mǎn le **shén mì,**shū zhōng miáo xiě
de nèi róng lìng tā men **jīng qí** yòu **jī dòng,**yīn cǐ zhè běn shū zài
dāng shí de ōu zhōu fēi cháng **liú xíng.**

马可·波罗叙述了中国的**辽阔**和**富有**、文化艺术的**繁荣**、工商业
的**发达**、交通运输的**完善方便**、建筑的**宏伟壮观**。他的游记中
描写了有着花园和**人造**湖泊的**华丽宫殿**，宽阔的**运河上川流不
息**的船只，**港口停泊**着大船，全国**纸币**的普及，**热闹**的**集市**有
各种**珍贵**的香料、丝绸、木料、食物、瓷器等等。他说自己很
快就学会了蒙古语和汉语，被忽必烈派往中国各地。每到一个
地方，马可·波罗都会仔细**考察**当地的**风俗民情**，并向忽必烈详
细**汇报**。他甚至还出国去到**越南**和**缅甸**。马可·波罗说的这一切
对当时的欧洲人来说，就像是神奇而古怪的故事，令人**难以置
信**，又无比**神往**。

mǎ kě •bō luó xù shù le zhōng guó de **liáo kuò** hé **fù yǒu,** wén huà
yì shù de **fán róng,** gōng shāng yè de **fā dá, jiāo tōng yùn shū** de
wán shàn fāng biàn, jiàn zhù de **hóng wěi zhuàng guān.** tā de yóu
jì zhōng miáo xiě le yǒu zhe huā yuán hé **rén zào** hú bó de **huá lì
gōng diàn,** kuān kuò de **yùn hé** shàng **chuān liú bú xī** de chuán zhī,
gǎng kǒu tíng bó zhe dà chuán, quán guó **zhǐ bì** de pǔjí, **rè nào** de
jí shì yǒu gè zhǒng **zhēn guì** de **xiāng liào, sī chóu, mù liào,** shí wù,
cí qì děng děng. tā shuō zì jǐ hěn kuài jiù xué huì le méng gǔ yǔ hé
hàn yǔ, bèi hū bì liè pài wǎng zhōng guó gè dì. měi dào yī gè dì
fāng,mǎ kě •bō luó dōu huì zī xì **kǎo chá** dāng dì de **fēng sú mín
qíng,** bìng xiàng hū bì liè xiáng xì **huì bào.** tā shèn zhì hái chū guó
qù dào **yuè nán** hé **miǎn diàn.** mǎ kě •bō luó shuō de zhè yī qiē duì
dāng shí de ōu zhōu rén lái shuō, jiù xiàng shì shén qí ér gǔ guài de
gù shì, lìng rén **nán yǐ zhì xìn,**yòu wú bǐ **shén wǎng.**

马可·波罗并不是第一个去中国的西方人，也不是第一个在中国**做官**的西方人，但他的游记让许多西方人了解中国和东方，**促进**了东西方的文化交流，也让后来的探险家们对东方产生了**兴趣**。因此它的作用十分重要。

mǎ kě •bō luó bìng bú shì dì yī gè qù zhōng guó de xī fāng rén, yě bú shì dì yī gè zài zhōng guó **zuò guān** de xī fāng rén, dàn tā de yóu jì ràng xǔ duō xī fāng rén liǎo jiě zhōng guó hé dōng fāng, **cù jìn** le dōng xī fāng de wén huà jiāo liú, yě ràng hòu lái de tàn xiǎn jiā men duì dōng fāng chǎn shēng le **xìng qù**. yīn cǐ tā de zuò yòng shí fèn zhòng yào.

有趣的是，据说意大利面并不是意大利人发明的，而是马可·波罗从中国把**面条**带到了意大利。**事实**是不是这样，也许**永远**也没人知道。不过中国人和意大利人都喜欢吃面条，你比较喜欢吃中国面条还是**意大利面**呢？

yǒu qù de shì,jù shuō yì dà lì miàn bìng bú shì yì dà lì rén fā míng de,ér shì mǎ kě •bō luó cóng zhōng guó bǎ **miàn tiáo** dài dào le yì dà lì. **shì shí** shì bú shì zhè yàng,yě xǔ **yǒng yuǎn** yě méi rén zhī dào. bú guò zhōng guó rén hé yì dà lì rén dōu xǐ huān chī miàn tiáo,nǐ bǐjiào xǐ huān chī zhōng guó miàn tiáo hái shì **yì dà lì miàn** ne?

总结（zǒng jié- Summary

十三世纪，马可·波罗从威尼斯去到中国，在元朝担任官职并生活了近二十年。回到意大利以后，他的经历被写成《马可·波罗游记》，让许多欧洲人第一次了解中国。

shí sān shì jì,mǎ kě •bō luó cóng wēi ní sī qù dào zhōng guó,zài yuán cháo dān rèn guān zhí bìng shēng huó le jìn èr shí nián. huí dào yì dà lì yǐ hòu,tā de jīng lì bèi xiě chéng <mǎ kě •bō luó yóu jì> ,ràng xǔ duō ōu zhōu rén dì yī cì liǎo jiě zhōng guó.

Summary of the story

Marco Polo, a merchant living in the 13th century Venice, travelled to China where it was ruled by the Yuan Dynasty. He was appointed to serve as the Khan's foreign emissary. After living in China for nearly 17 years, Marco Polo went back to Italy. The stories he told were recorded, known as the book The Travels of Marco Polo, which allowed many people in Europe to know about China for the first time.

Vocabulary

- 意大利 **(yì dà lì)**: Italy
- 悠久 **(yōu jiǔ)**: long, long-standing
- 历史 **(lì shǐ)**: History
- 深厚 **(shēn hòu)**: deep and rich
- 文化 **(wén huà)**: Culture
- 代表 **(dài biǎo)**: to represent
- 影响力 **(yǐng xiǎng lì)**: influence
- 东方 **(dōng fāng)**: the Orient, the East
- 文明 **(wén míng)**: civilization
- 传承 **(chuán chéng)**: inherit
- 古罗马 **(gǔ luó mǎ)**: the ancient Rome
- 辉煌 **(huī huáng)**: splendid
- 遗产 **(yí chǎn)**: legacy, heritage
- 友好 **(yǒu hǎo)**: friendly
- 频繁 **(pín fán)**: frequent, frequently
- 旅游 **(lǚ yóu)**: to travel
- 游记 **(yóu jì)**: travel notes, stories
- 马可·波罗 **(mǎ kě•bō luó)**: Marco Polo
- 威尼斯 **(wēi ní sī)**: Venice
- 商业 **(shāng yè)**: commercial business, trades
- 兴盛 **(xīng shèng)**: prosperous
- 远东 **(yuǎn dōng)**: the Far East
- 做生意 **(zuò shēng yì)**: do business, trade
- 蒙古 **(méng gǔ)**: Mongolia
- 统治者 **(tǒng zhì zhě)**: the ruler
- 元朝 **(yuán cháo)**: the Yuan Dynasty
- 皇帝 **(huáng dì)**: emperor
- 忽必烈 **(hū bì liè)**: Kublai

- 教皇 (jiào huáng): the Pope
- 担任 (dān rèn): take a position
- 官职 (guān zhí): government post
- 欧洲 (ōu zhōu): Europe
- 战争 (zhàn zhēng): war
- 俘虏 (fú lǔ): captive, war prisoner
- 监狱 (jiān yù): prison
- 经历 (jīng lì): experience
- 描述 (miáo shù): description
- 见闻 (jiàn wén): what one sees and hears
- 介绍 (jiè shào): introduction
- 有限 (yǒu xiàn): limited
- 神秘 (shén mì): mysterious
- 惊奇 (jīng qí): surprised
- 激动 (jī dòng): excited
- 流行 (liú xíng): popular
- 辽阔 (liáo kuò): vast, expansive
- 富有 (fù yǒu): rich, abundant
- 繁荣 (fán róng): prosperous
- 发达 (fā dá): advanced
- 交通 (jiāo tōng): traffic, transportation
- 运输 (yùn shū): transport
- 完善 (wán shàn): comprehensive, complete
- 方便 (fāng biàn): convenient
- 宏伟壮观 (hóng wěi zhuàng guān): magnificent, spectacular
- 人造 (rén zào): man-made, artificial
- 华丽 (huá lì): gorgeous, splendid
- 宫殿 (gōng diàn): palace
- 运河 (yùn hé): canal
- 川流不息 (chuān liú bú xī): coming and going in an endless flow
- 港口 (gǎng kǒu): harbor, port

- 停泊 (tíng bó): anchor at, dock
- 纸币 (zhǐ bì): banknote, paper money
- 热闹 (rè nào): bustling with noise and excitement
- 集市 (jí shì): market fair, bazaar
- 珍贵 (zhēn guì): precious
- 香料 (xiāng liào): spices
- 丝绸 (sī chóu): silk
- 木料 (mù liào): timber, lumber
- 瓷器 (cí qì): chinaware
- 考察 (kǎo chá): observe and study, investigate
- 风俗 (fēng sú): customs
- 民情 (mín qíng): conditions of the people
- 汇报 (huì bào): report (in a compiled summary)
- 越南 (yuè nán): Vietnam
- 缅甸 (miǎn diàn): Myanmar
- 难以置信 (nán yǐ zhì xìn): incredible, unbelievable
- 神往 (shén wǎng): be charmed, be carried away
- 做官 (zuò guān): serve an official position
- 促进 (cù jìn): facilitate, promote
- 兴趣 (xìng qù): interest
- 面条 (miàn tiáo): noodles
- 事实 (shì shí): facts
- 永远 (yǒng yuan): forever
- 意大利面 (yì dà lì miàn): pasta

Questions about the story

1. 马可·波罗是哪个国家的人？

   mǎ kě·bō luó shì nǎ ge guó jiā de rén?

   a) 中国

      zhōng guó

   b) 意大利

      yì dà lì

   c) 蒙古

      méng gǔ

2. 马可·波罗为什么去中国？

   mǎ kě·bō luó wèi shé me qù zhōng guó?

   a) 作为教皇的使者

      zuò wéi jiào huáng de shǐ zhě

   b) 为了做生意

      wèi le zuò shēng yì

   c) 为了探险

      wèi le tàn xiǎn

3. 关于《马可·波罗游记》的说法，哪个是正确的？

   guān yú "mǎ kě·bō luó yóu jì" de shuō fǎ, nǎ ge shì zhèng què de?

   a) 游记是马可·波罗本人写的

      yóu jì shì mǎ kě·bō luó běn rén xiě de

   b) 游记是马可·波罗在中国的时候写的

      yóu jì shì mǎ kě·bō luó zài zhōng guó de shí hòu xiě de

c) 游记在欧洲非常流行

    yóu jì zài ōu zhōu fēi cháng liú xíng

4. 下面哪一个不是《马可·波罗游记》中的内容？

   xià miàn nǎ yī gè bù shì "mǎ kě·bō luó yóu jì" zhōng de nèi róng?

    a) 中国清朝的皇帝

       zhōng guó qīng cháo de huáng dì

    b) 中国元朝的宫殿

       zhōng guó yuán cháo de gōng diàn

    c) 中国元朝的集市

       zhōng guó yuán cháo de jí shì

5. 马可·波罗没有去过的国家是？

   mǎ kě·bō luó méi yǒu qù guò de guó jiā shì?

    a) 美国

       měi guó

    b) 中国

       zhōng guó

    c) 越南

       yuè nán

Answers

1. B
2. A
3. C
4. A
5. A

Chapter IV

十二生肖 (SHÍ ÈR SHĒNG XIĀO)

很多人都知道十二**星座**，但你知道吗，在中国文化里还有十二**生肖**。有十二种**动物**，它们按照**顺序排列**，随着农历新年的到来做**轮换**，因此每一年都有**对应**的**象征**动物，每十二年为一个**周期**。比如2020年的**春节**过后，接下来的一年就是**鼠年**，这一年的生肖是老鼠。下一次的鼠年就是2032年。

hěn duō rén dōu zhī dào shí èr **xīng zuò,** dàn nǐ zhī dào ma, zài zhōng guó wén huà lǐ hái yǒu shí èr **shēng xiāo.** yo shí èr zhǒng **dòng wù,** tā men àn zhào **shùn xù pái liè,** suí zhe nóng lì xīn nián de dào lái zuò **lún huàn,** yīn cǐ měi yī nián dōu yǒu **duì yìng** de **xiàng zhēng** dòng wù, měi shí èr nián wéi yī gè **zhōu qī.** bǐ rú 2020 nián de **chūn jié** guò hòu, jiē xià lái de yī nián jiù shì **shǔ nián,** zhè yī nián de shēng xiāo shì lǎo shǔ. xià yī cì de shǔ nián jiù shì 2032 nián.

生肖在中国有着非常悠久的历史。**考古**发现的**秦代文物**里就有相关**记载**，那是一千五百多年前。这十二种动物**依次**是：鼠、牛、虎、兔、龙、蛇、马、羊、猴、鸡、狗，和猪。生肖也叫**属相**，某一年里出生的人的属相就是这一年的生肖动物。比如2020年春节到2021年春节之间出生的人的属相就是老鼠，也可以说他们属鼠。接下去一年**出生**的人则属牛。

shēng xiāo zài zhōng guó yǒu zhe fēi cháng yōu jiǔ de lì shǐ. **kǎo gǔ** fā xiàn de **qín dài wén wù** lǐ jiù yǒu xiàng guān **jì zǎi**, nà shì yī qiān wǔ bǎi duō nián qián. zhè shí èr zhǒng dòng wù **yī cì** shì: shǔ, niú, hǔ, tù, lóng, shé, mǎ, yáng, hóu, jī, gǒu, hé zhū. shēng xiāo yě jiào **shǔ xiàng**, mǒu yī nián lǐ chū shēng de rén de shǔ xiàng jiù shì zhè yī nián de shēng xiāo dòng wù. bǐ rú 2020 nián chūn jiē dào 2021 nián chūn jiē zhī jiān chū shēng de rén de shǔ xiàng jiù shì lǎo shǔ, yě kě yǐ shuō tā men shǔ shǔ. jiē xià qù yī nián **chū shēng** de rén zé shǔ niú.

和星座一样,在中国的传统文化里,每种生肖所对应属相的人,也被认为具有各自的**性格**和**能力特征**。这些特征有的和生肖动物相关,比如:属鼠的人**直觉敏锐**,属牛的人**勤奋**而**顽固**,属兔的人**温和细心**,属龙的人喜欢**冒险**,等等......也会有人用生肖来**占卜**:属虎的人今年**运气**不错,属鸡的人今年可能会**生病**,属猴的人或许会**结婚**......这些说法准确吗?就像星座占卜,也许准,也许不准。有的人相信,有的人不信。不如把它当成一种趣味文化吧。

hé xīng zuò yī yàng, zài zhōng guó de chuán tǒng wén huà lǐ, měi zhǒng shēng xiāo suǒ duì yīng shǔ xiàng de rén, yě bèi rèn wéi jù yǒu gè zì de **xìng gé** hé **néng lì tè zhēng**. zhè xiē tè zhēng yǒu de hé shēng xiāo dòng wù xiàng guān, bǐ rú: shǔ shǔ de rén **zhí jué mǐn ruì**, shǔ niú de rén **qín fèn** ér **wán gù**, shǔ tù de rén **wēn hé xì xīn**, shǔ lóng de rén xǐ huān **mào xiǎn**, děng děng......yě huì yǒu rén yòng shēng xiāo lái **zhàn bǔ**: shǔ hǔ de rén jīn nián **yùn qì** bú cuò, shǔ jī de rén jīn nián kě néng huì **shēng bìng**, shǔ hóu de rén huò xǔ huì **jié hūn**......zhè xiē shuō fǎ zhǔn què ma? jiù xiàng xīng zuò zhàn bǔ, yě xǔ zhǔn, yě xǔ bú zhǔn. yǒu de rén xiàng xìn, yǒu de rén bú xìn. bú rú bǎ tā dāng chéng yī zhǒng qù wèi wén huà ba.

在这十二种动物里,老鼠没有牛**强壮**,没有老虎**勇猛**,不会像马那样**奔驰**，也没有龙的**神奇力量**，就连在**日常生活**中，老鼠也不如狗、猪、羊、鸡对人类有用。那么为什么老鼠会在十二生肖中排在**第一位**呢？关于这个，有一个有趣的传说。

zài zhè shí èr zhǒng dòng wù lǐ, lǎo shǔ méi yǒu niú **qiáng zhuàng**, méi yǒu lǎo hǔ **yǒng měng**, bú huì xiàng mǎ nà yàng **bēn chí**, yě méi yǒu lóng de **shén qí lì liàng**, jiù lián zài **rì cháng shēng huó** zhōng, lǎo shǔ yě bù rú gǒu, zhū, yáng, jī duì rén lèi yǒu yòng. nà me wéi shí me lǎo shǔ huì zài shí èr shēng xiāo zhōng pái zài **dì yī wèi** ne? guān yú zhè gè, yǒu yī gè yǒu qù de chuán shuō.

天上的**神仙**选定了十二种动物作为生肖，让它们自己**商量**如何**排位**。因为老黄牛**勤劳宽厚**，连龙和虎也尊敬它，因此大家都**同意**让它排第一。只有老鼠**反对**，说："我才是最大，不信的话我们去**人间**走走，看看**百姓**怎么说。"于是，牛和老鼠一起来到了人间。它们到了一条热闹的街道，牛从街上的**人群**中走过，人们都觉得很平常，没有什么特别的**反应**。这时候，老鼠一下子爬到牛背上，再爬到牛**角**上，**站立**起来。人们大为惊讶，**纷纷**说："看啊，好大的老鼠！"于是老鼠**得意**地说："果然还是我最大吧。"其他动物只好**无奈**地答应了。

tiān shàng de **shén xiān** xuǎn dìng le shí èr zhǒng dòng wù zuò wéi shēng xiāo, ràng tā men zì jǐ **shāng liáng** rú hé **pái wèi**. yīn wéi lǎo huáng niú **qín láo kuān hòu**, lián lóng hé hǔ yě zūn jìng tā, yīn cǐ dà jiā dōu **tóng yì** ràng tā pái dì yī. zhī yǒu lǎo shǔ **fǎn duì**, shuō: "wǒ cái shì zuì dà, bú xìn dehuà wǒ men qù **rén jiān** zǒu zǒu, kàn kàn **bǎi xìng** zěn me shuō. "yú shì, niú hé lǎo shǔ yī qǐ lái dào le rén jiān. tā men dào le yī tiáo rè nào de jiē dào, niú cóng jiē shàng de **rén qún** zhōng zǒu guò, rén men dōu jué dé hěn píng cháng, méi yǒu shí me tè bié de **fǎn yìng**. zhè shí hòu, lǎo shǔ yī xià zǐ pá dào niú bèi shàng, zài pá dào niú **jiǎo** shàng, **zhàn lì** qǐ lái. rén men dà wéi jīng yà, **fēn fēn** shuō: "kàn ā, hǎo dà de lǎo shǔ" yú shì lǎo shǔ **dé yì** dì shuō: "guǒ rán hái shì wǒ zuì dà ba." qí tā dòng wù zhǐ hǎo **wú nài** dì dá yīng le.

每一年农历新年时，在中国**到处**都能看到那一年的生肖动物**图案**。它们以各种各样的**设计**被贴在人们家里的门窗上，用在**服装**设计和**礼物包装**上，还经常出现在**电视节目**里，成为那一年的**明星**动物。

měi yī nián nóng lì xīn nián shí, zài zhōng guó **dào chù** dōu néng kàn dào nà yī nián de shēng xiāo dòng wù **tú àn**. tā men yǐ gè zhǒng gè yàng de **shè jì** bèi tiē zài rén men jiā lǐ de mén chuāng shàng, yòng zài **fú zhuāng** shè jì hé **lǐ wù bāo zhuāng** shàng, hái jīng cháng chū xiàn zài **diàn shì jié mù** lǐ, chéng wéi nà yī nián de **míng xīng** dòng wù.

总结 （zǒng jié- Summary

在中国传统文化中，十二生肖是十二种具有象征意义的动物，每年轮流替换。每一年出生的人的属相就是那种动物，并且被认为具有生肖动物的特征。关于老鼠在生肖中排名第一，有一个有趣的传说。

zài zhōng guó chuán tǒng wén huà zhōng, shí èr shēng xiāo shì shí èr zhǒng jù yǒu xiàng zhēng yì yì de dòng wù, měi nián lún liú tì huàn. měi yī nián chū shēng de rén de shǔ xiàng jiù shì nà zhǒng dòng wù, bìng qiě bèi rèn wéi jù yǒu shēng xiāo dòng wù de tè zhēng. guān yú lǎo shǔ zài shēng xiāo zhōng pái míng dì yī, yǒu yī gè yǒu qù de chuán shuō.

Summary of the story

In the Chinese traditional culture, the twelve Chinese zodiac signs are represented by twelve animals. Every year there is a different animal. People born in a year have their zodiac animal of the year, and are believed to have unique features associated with that animal. How did the rat rank first among all the zodiac animals? There is an interesting story about that.

Vocabulary

- 星座 (xīng zuò): horoscope
- 生肖 (shēng xiāo): Chinese zodiac signs
- 动物 (dòng wù): animal
- 顺序 (shùn xù): sequence
- 排列 (pái liè): rank in order
- 轮换 (lún huàn): rotate, take turns
- 对应 (duì yìng): corresponding
- 象征 (xiàng zhēng): symbol
- 周期 (zhōu qī): cycle
- 春节 (chūn jié): the Chinese New Year, Spring Festival
- 鼠年 (shǔ nián): year of rat
- 考古 (kǎo gǔ): archaeology
- 秦代 (qín dài): the Qin Dynasty
- 文物 (wén wù): cultural relic
- 记载 (jì zǎi): record
- 依次 (yī cì): in proper order, successively
- 属相 (shǔ xiàng): the symbolic animal of the Chinese zodiac signs
- 出生 (chū shēng): be born
- 性格 (xìng gé): personality
- 能力 (néng lì): capability
- 特征 (tè zhēng): feature, characteristic
- 直觉 (zhí jué): intuition
- 敏锐 (mǐn ruì): acute, sharp
- 勤奋 (qín fèn): diligent
- 顽固 (wán gù): stubborn
- 温和 (wēn hé): gentle
- 细心 (xì xīn): careful, attentive
- 冒险 (mào xiǎn): adventure

- **占卜 (zhàn bǔ):** fortune telling, practise divination
- **运气 (yùn qì):** fortune
- **生病 (shēng bìng):** fall ill, become sick
- **结婚 (jié hūn):** get married
- **强壮 (qiáng zhuàng):** strong
- **勇猛 (yǒng měng):** bold and powerful
- **奔驰 (bēn chí):** gallop, run fast
- **神奇 (shén qí):** magical, miraculous
- **力量 (lì liàng):** power
- **日常生活 (rì cháng shēng huó):** daily life
- **第一位 (dì yī wèi):** the first place
- **神仙 (shén xiān):** the immortal, the celestial being
- **商量 (shāng liáng):** to discuss, to talk over
- **排位 (pái wèi):** set the rank
- **勤劳 (qín láo):** diligent, hardworking
- **宽厚 (kuān hòu):** generous, lenient
- **同意 (tóng yì):** agree, support
- **反对 (fǎn duì):** disagree, be against
- **人间 (rén jiān):** man's world
- **百姓 (bǎi xìng):** the common people
- **人群 (rén qún):** a crowd of people
- **反应 (fǎn yìng):** reaction
- **角 (jiǎo):** horn
- **站立 (zhàn lì):** stand up
- **纷纷 (fēn fēn):** one after another, numerous
- **得意 (dé yì):** feeling complacent
- **无奈 (wú nài):** have no alternative
- **到处 (dào chù):** everywhere

43

- **图案 (tú àn):** pattern, image
- **设计 (shè jì):** design
- **服装 (fú zhuāng):** clothing
- **礼物 (lǐ wù):** gift, present
- **包装 (bāo zhuāng):** wrapping, packaging
- **电视 (diàn shì):** television
- **节目 (jié mù):** programme
- **明星 (míng xīng):** star

Questions about the story

1. 十二生肖中排第一的是？

   shí èr shēng xiào zhōng pái dì yī de shì?

   a) 龙
      lóng

   b) 牛
      niú

   c) 鼠
      shǔ

2. 关于十二生肖的说法里，正确的是？

   guān yú shí èr sheng xiào de shuō fǎ lǐ, zhèng què de shì?

   a) 是中国传统文化的一部分
      shì zhōng guó chuán tǒng wén huà de yī bù fèn

   b) 是现代才出现的
      shì xiàn dài cái chū xiàn de

   c) 是由十二种花组成的
      shì yóu shí èr zhòng huā zǔ chéng de

3. 生肖每隔多久换一次？

   shēng xiào měi gé duō jiǔ huàn yīcì?

   a) 一个月
      yī gè yuè

   b) 一年
      yī nián

   c) 十二年
      shí èr nián

4. 传说中，老鼠是怎么成为十二生肖之首的？

   chuán shuō zhōng, lǎo shǔ shì zěn me chéng wéi shí èr

   sheng xiào zhī shǒu de?

   a) 被神仙指定的

      bèi shén xiān zhǐ dìng de

   b) 由其他动物推选的

      yóu qí tā dòng wù tuī xuǎn de

   c) 通过耍花招

      tōng guò shuǎ huā zhāo

5. 下面哪种动物不是十二生肖中的？

   xià miàn nǎ zhǒng dòng wù bù shì shí èr sheng xiào zhōng

   de?

   a) 鸡

      jī

   b) 猫

      māo

   c) 蛇

      shé

Answers

1. C
2. A
3. B
4. C
5. B

Chapter V

三个和尚 (SĀN GÈ HÉ SHÀNG)

从前有一座山，山上有一座没有人住的庙。有一天，一个年轻的小和尚来到这里，决定在庙里住下来。庙里的水缸里没有水，山上也没有水井。于是他一个人背着水桶到山下，在水井里装满了一桶水，再背上山。他烧水做饭，也把水倒进了佛像前的瓶子里，插进带着绿叶的树枝，供奉菩萨。就这样，他每天下山背水，做饭，在庙里念经，敲木鱼，生活得平静而满足。

cóng qián yǒu yī zuò **shān**, shān shàng yǒu yī zuò méi yǒu rén zhù de **miào**. yǒu yī tiān, yī gè **nián qīng** de xiǎo **hé shàng** lái dào zhè lǐ, jué dìng zài miào lǐ zhù xià lái. miào lǐ de **shuǐ gāng** lǐ méi yǒu shuǐ, shān shàng yě méi yǒu **shuǐ jǐng**. yú shì tā yī gè rén **bēi** zhe shuǐ **tǒng** dào shān xià, zài shuǐ jǐng lǐ **zhuāng** mǎn le yī tǒng shuǐ, zài bēi shàng shān. tā **shāo shuǐ zuò fàn**, yě bǎ shuǐ **dǎo jìn** le **fó xiàng** qián de **píng zǐ** lǐ, **chā** jìn dài zhe **lǜ yè** de **shù zhī**, **gòng fèng pú sà**. jiù zhè yàng, tā měi tiān xià shān bēi shuǐ, zuò fàn, zài miào lǐ **niàn jīng**, **qiāo mù yú**, shēng huó dé **píng jìng** ér **mǎn zú**.

有一天，有一个高个子的和尚来到庙里。他也是旅行路过这里，见到这座庙和庙里的小和尚，觉得这里不错，于是也想住下来。矮和尚也觉得一个人有些寂寞，很高兴有人作伴。高和尚走了很久，非常口渴，就从水缸里一口气喝了很多水。小和尚告诉他水井在山下，要高和尚下山去背水。可是高和尚说："今后我们一起住在这里，我一个人去背水不**公平**，应该两个人一起去。"矮和尚觉得他说得**有道理**，只好同意了。

yǒu yī tiān, yǒu yī gè **gāo gè zǐ** de hé shàng lái dào miào lǐ. tā yě shì lǚ xíng **lù guò** zhè lǐ, jiàn dào zhè zuò miào hé miào lǐ de xiǎo hé shàng, jué dé zhè lǐ bú cuò, yú shì yě xiǎng zhù xià lái. ǎi hé shàng yě jué dé yī gè rén yǒu xiē **jì mò**, hěn **gāo xìng** yǒu rén **zuò bàn**. gāo hé shàng zǒu le **hěn jiǔ**, fēi cháng **kǒu kě**, jiù cóng shuǐ gāng lǐ **yī kǒu qì** hē le hěn duō shuǐ. xiǎo hé shàng gào sù tā shuǐ jǐng zài shān xià, yào gāo hé shàng xià shān qù bēi shuǐ. kě shì gāo hé shàng shuō: "**jīn hòu** wǒ men yī qǐ zhù zài zhè lǐ, wǒ yī gè rén qù bēi shuǐ bú **gōng píng**, yīng gāi liǎng gè rén yī qǐ qù. " ǎi hé shàng jué dé tā shuō dé **yǒu dào lǐ**, zhī hǎo tóng yì le.

他们在庙外面**砍**了一株**竹子**，把**树干**做成**扁担**，用来**挑**水桶。小和尚走在**前面**，高和尚走在**后面**。只要水桶往前或者往后**偏移**一点，走在前面或者后面的人就会觉得不公平，要**停**下来把水桶移回到扁担中间，才能**继续**走。就这样，一路上走走停停，两个人挑水所**花**的时间**比**一个人背水还要**多很多**。而且他们心里都**认为对方**是**故意偷懒**，想让自己多花**力气**。时间一天天过去，他们心里的**不满越来越**多，**有时候会吵架**。但他们还是每天一起下山挑水，因为谁也不愿意自己一个人**干活**，让另一个人白白喝水。他们在庙里**各**自念经、敲木鱼，谁也不**理睬**谁。因为用在挑水和争吵上的时间变多，他们供奉菩萨的时间变少了，**心情**也不愉快。

tā men zài miào wài miàn **kǎn** le yī zhū **zhú zǐ**, bǎ **shù gàn** zuò chéng **biǎn dàn**, yòng lái **tiāo** shuǐ tǒng. xiǎo hé shàng zǒu zài **qián miàn**, gāo hé shàng zǒu zài **hòu miàn**. zhī yào shuǐ tǒng wǎng qián huò zhě wǎng hòu **piān yí** yī diǎn, zǒu zài qián miàn huò zhě hòu miàn de rén jiù huì jué dé bú gōng píng, yào **tíng** xià lái bǎ shuǐ

49

tǒng yí huí dào biǎn dàn zhōng jiān, cái néng **jì xù** zǒu. jiù zhè yàng, yī lù shàng zǒu zǒu tíng tíng, liǎng gè rén tiāo shuǐ suǒ **huā** de shí jiān **bǐ** yī gè rén bēi shuǐ hái yào **duō hen duō**. ér qiě tā men xīn lǐ dōu **rèn wéi duì fāng** shì gù yì tōu lǎn, xiǎng ràng zì jǐ duō huā **lì qì**. shí jiān yī tiān tiān guò qù, tā men xīn lǐ de **bù mǎn yuè lái yuè** duō, **yǒu shí hòu** huì **chǎo jià**. dàn tā men hái shì měi tiān yī qǐ xià shān tiāo shuǐ, yīn wéi shuí yě bú yuàn yì zì jǐ yī gè rén **gàn huó,** ràng lìng yī gè rén **bái bái** hē shuǐ. tā men zài miào lǐ **gè zì** niàn jīng, qiāo mù yú, shuí yě bú **lǐ cǎi** shuí. yīn wéi yòng zài tiāo shuǐ hé zhēng chǎo shàng de shí jiān biàn duō, tā men gòng fèng pú sà de shí jiān biàn shǎo le, **xīn qíng** yě bú yú kuài.

这样过了一段时间，又来了一个胖和尚。他也喜欢上了这个庙，决定住下来。刚好水缸里没水了，小和尚和高和尚互看了一眼，就对胖和尚说："你是新来的，你去挑水。"胖和尚知道他们是在欺负自己，也不说话，就背起水桶下山去了。等他把水背上山，就自己全喝光了，一点也没留给另外两个人。另外两个和尚气坏了，三个人大吵了一架，谁也不愿意再去挑水，佛像前的瓶子里没有水，树枝也干枯了。

zhè yàng guò le yī duàn shí jiān, yòu lái le yī gè **pàng** hé shàng. tā yě xǐ huān shàng le zhè gè miào, jué dìng zhù xià lái. gāng hǎo shuǐ gāng lǐ méi shuǐ le, xiǎo hé shàng hé gāo hé shàng hù kàn le yī yǎn, jiù duì pàng hé shàng shuō: "nǐ shì **xīn lái de**, nǐ qù tiāo shuǐ. "pàng hé shàng zhī dào tā men shì zài **qī fù** zì jǐ, yě bú shuō huà, jiù bēi qǐ shuǐ tǒng xià shān qù le. děng tā bǎ shuǐ bēi shàng shān, jiù zì jǐ quán hē guāng le, yī diǎn yě méi **liú gěi** lìng wài liǎng gè rén. lìng wài liǎng gè hé shàng qì huài le, sān gè rén **dà chǎo le yī jià**, shuí yě bú yuàn yì zài qù tiāo shuǐ, fó xiàng qián de píng zǐ lǐ méi yǒu shuǐ, shù zhī yě **gān kū** le.

那天夜里，有一只老鼠出来**偷**东西吃。三个和尚都听到了声音，可是谁也不想**管**。老鼠**爬**上桌子，**撞倒了蜡烛**，**烧着了桌布**，**燃起**了大火。可是这时候庙里没有水了。三个和尚**慌**了，**轮流**跑下山去打水，**终于**一起努力**扑灭**了火。他们这才**明白**，人多不一定是好事，还要努力**协作**。

nà tiān yè lǐ, yǒu yī zhī lǎo shǔ chū lái **tōu** dōng xī chī. sān gè hé shàng dōu tīng dào le shēng yīn, kě shì shuí yě bú xiǎng **guǎn**. lǎo shǔ **pá** shàng zhuō zǐ, **zhuàng dǎo** le **là zhú**, **shāo zhaó** le **zhuō bù**, **rán qǐ** le dà huǒ. kě shì zhè shí hòu miào lǐ méi yǒu shuǐ le. sān gè hé shàng **huāng** le, **lún liú** pǎo xià shān qù dǎ shuǐ, **zhōng yú** yī qǐ nǔ lì **pū miè** le huǒ. tā men zhè cái **míng bái**, rén duō bú yī dìng shì hǎo shì, hái yào nǔ lì **xié zuò**.

总结 （zng jié- Summary

一个和尚来到了一座没有人的庙里生活，自己下山背水，生活得平静而满足。第二个和尚来了，两个人一起挑水，时间更长，争吵更多。第三个和尚来了，三个和尚没水喝。为什么会这样？人多不一定力量大。

yī gè hé shàng lái dào le yī zuò méi yǒu rén de miào lǐ shēng huó, zì jǐ xià shān bēi shuǐ shēng huó dé píng jìng ér mǎn zú. dì èr gè hé shàng lái le, liǎng gè rén yī qǐ tiāo shuǐ, shí jiān gèng zhǎng, zhēng chǎo gèng duō. dì sān gè hé shàng lái le, sān gè hé shàng méi shuǐ hē. wéi shí me huì zhè yàng? rén duō bú yī dìng lì liàng dà.

Summary of the story

A monk came to live in a temple on the hill. He goes downhill to fetch water and feels content. A second monk came. They share the water-carrying task everyday. It now takes more time and makes them argue with each other. A third monk's arrival led to a big fight. No water was left for anyone and nobody wanted to fetch water. How did this happen? More people doesn't necessarily mean better results.

Vocabulary

- **从前 (cóng qián)**: once upon a time
- **山 (shān)**: hill, mountain
- **庙 (miào)**: temple
- **年轻 (nián qīng)**: young, adolescent
- **和尚 (hé shàng)**: monk
- **水缸 (shuǐ gāng)**: water jar, water vat
- **水井 (shuǐ jǐng)**: water well
- **背 (bēi)**: to carry on the back
- **桶 (tǒng)**: barrel, bucket
- **装 (zhuāng)**: to fill with, put inside
- **烧水 (shāo shuǐ)**: to boil some water
- **做饭 (zuò fàn)**: to cook a meal
- **倒进 (dǎo jìn)**: to pour inside
- **佛像 (fó xiàng)**: figure or statue of the Buddha

- **瓶子 (píng zǐ)**: bottle
- **插 (chā)**: to insert, stick in
- **绿叶 (lǜ yè)**: green leaves
- **树枝 (shù zhī)**: twig, tree branch
- **供奉 (gòng fèng)**: to enshrine and worship
- **菩萨 (pú sà)**: Bodhisattva
  念经 (niàn jīng): to recite or chant scriptures or mantras
- **敲木鱼 (qiāo mù yú)**: to knock on a wooden fish
- **平静 (píng jìng)**: feeling calm, in peace
- **满足 (mǎn zú)**: feeling content
- **高个子 (gāo gè zǐ)**: (person) tall
- **路过 (lù guò)**: pass by
- **寂寞 (jì mò)**: feeling lonely
- **高兴 (gāo xìng)**: happy, glad

- 作伴 (zuò bàn): to have companion
- 很久 (hěn jiǔ): for a long time
- 口渴 (kǒu kě): feeling thirsty
- 一口气 (yī kǒu qì): in one breath, without a break
- 今后 (jīn hòu): from now on
- 公平 (gōng píng): fair, just
- 有道理 (yǒu dào lǐ): making sense, reasonable
- 砍 (kǎn): to chop, to hack
- 竹子 (zhú zǐ): bamboo
- 树干 (shù gàn): tree trunk
- 扁担 (biǎn dàn): a carrying pole put on the shoulders
- 挑 (tiāo): to tote with a carrying pole
- 前面 (qián miàn): at the front, forward, before
- 后面 (hòu miàn): at the back, backward, behind
- 偏移 (piān yí): to shift, to move to deviate from
- 停 (tíng): to stop, to halt
- 继续 (jì xù): to continue
- 花 (huā): to spend, to consume
- 比……多很多 (bǐ…… duō hen duō): much more than
- 认为 (rèn wéi): to think, to believe
- 对方 (duì fāng): the other party, the opposite party
- 故意 (gù yì): on purpose, intentionally
- 偷懒 (tōu lǎn): to loaf on the job
- 力气 (lì qì): efforts, strengths
- 不满 (bù mǎn): feeling discontented, resentful
- 越来越 (yuè lái yuè): more and more
- 有时候 (yǒu shí hòu): sometimes
- 吵架 (chǎo jià): to quarrel, to have a row

- 干活 (**gàn huó**): to work, do a job
- 白白 (**bái bái**): for nothing, getting something without paying efforts
- 各自 (**gè zì**): each, separately
- 理睬 (**lǐ cǎi**): to pay attention to, to react to, to show interest in
- 心情 (**xīn qíng**): mood, state of mind
- 胖 (**pàng**): fat
- 新来的 (**xīn lái de**): someone who's newly arrived
- 欺负 (**qī fù**): to bully
- 留给 (**liú gěi**): save something for someone
- 大吵一架 (**dà chǎo le yī jià**): to have a big verbal fight
- 干枯 (**gān kū**): to dry up, to wither

- 偷 (**tōu**): to steal
- 管 (**guǎn**): to take care of, to manage
- 爬 (**pá**): to crawl, to climb
- 撞倒 (**zhuàng dǎo**): to knock something over
- 蜡烛 (**là zhú**): candle
- 烧着 (**shāo zhaó**): to catch fire
- 桌布 (**zhuō bù**): table cloth
- 燃起 (**rán qǐ**): to burn
- 慌 (**huāng**): to panic
- 轮流 (**lún liú**): to take turns, to do something in turn
- 终于 (**zhōng yú**): finally
- 扑灭 (**pū miè**): to put out a fire
- 明白 (**míng bái**): to realize
- 协作 (**xié zuò**): to coordinate

Questions about the story

1. 最先住进庙里的是？

   zuì xiān zhù jìn miào lǐ de shì?

   a) 小和尚

   　　xiǎo hé shàng

   b) 高个子和尚

   　　gāo gè zi hé shàng

   c) 胖和尚

   　　pàng hé shàng

2. 庙里有两个和尚的时候，是怎么取水的？

   miào li yǒu liǎng gè hé shàng de shí hòu, shì zěn me qǔ shuǐ
   de?

   a) 由小和尚下山去背水

   　　yóu xiǎo hé shàng xià shān qù bēi shuǐ

   b) 两个人轮流下山去背水

   　　liǎng gè rén lún liú xià shān qù bēi shuǐ

   c) 两个人一起下山挑水

   　　liǎng gè rén yī qǐ xià shān tiāo shuǐ

3. 下列说法中正确的是：

   xià liè shuō fǎ zhōng zhèng què de shì:

   a) 山上就有水井

   　　shān shàng jiù yǒu shuǐ jǐng

   b) 高个子的和尚是路过这座庙的

   　　gāo gè zi de hé shàng shì lù guò zhè zuò miào de

56

c) 小和尚拒绝让高个子和尚住在庙里

xiǎo hé shàng jù jué ràng gāo gè zi hé shàng zhù zài miào lǐ

4. 庙里是怎么发生火灾的？

miào lǐ shì zěn me fā shēng huǒ zāi de?

a) 因为三个和尚吵架

yīn wèi sān gè hé shàng chǎo jià

b) 因为菩萨惩罚

yīn wèi púsà chéng fá

c) 因为老鼠撞倒了蜡烛

yīn wèi lǎo shǔ zhuàng dǎo le là zhú

5. 关于这个故事的含义，下面哪种说法是错的？

guān yú zhè ge gùshì de hán yì, xià miàn nǎ zhǒng shuō fǎ shì

cuò de?

a) 人越多，事情越容易做好

rén yuè duō, shì qíng yuè róng yì zuò hǎo

b) 人多未必能办好事情

rén duō wèi bì néng bàn hǎo shì qíng

c) 协同合作非常重要

xié tóng hé zuò fēi cháng zhòng yào

Answers

1. A
2. C
3. B
4. C
5. A

Chapter VI

屋檐下的燕子
(WŪ YÁN XIÀ DE YÀN ZǏ)

有一个十岁的小女孩，她的**名字**叫小燕，住在中国**北方**的一座**城市**。**燕子**是一种鸟，这个叫小燕的女孩就**像飞来飞去**的燕子一样，**活泼**又**灵巧**，爱唱歌也爱跳舞。尤其是一头黑黑的**长发**扎成两条**辫子**，跳舞的时候就飞起来，就像燕子的**翅膀**。

yǒu yī gè shí suì de xiǎo nǚ hái, tā de **míng zì** jiào xiǎo yàn, zhù zài zhōng guó **běi fāng** de yī zuò **chéng shì**. **yàn zǐ** shì yī zhǒng niǎo, zhè gè jiào xiǎo yàn de nǚ hái jiù **xiàng fēi lái fēi qù** de yàn zǐ yī yàng, **huó pō** yòu **líng qiǎo**, ài chàng gē yě ài tiào wǔ. yóu qí shì yī tóu hēi hēi de **cháng fā zhā** chéng liǎng tiáo **biàn zǐ**, tiào wǔ de shí hòu jiù fēi qǐ lái, jiù xiàng yàn zǐ de **chì bǎng**.

去年夏天，小燕发现**门口**的**屋檐**下有一个燕子**窝**，**邻居**们都说这象征着**吉利**。燕子窝里住着两只小燕子，它们很**可爱**。黑色的**羽毛**，白色的**肚皮**，一双**灵活**的小**眼睛**，像一对**黑亮**的**宝石**，**剪刀**似的**尾巴**，好像身穿一件**燕尾服**，漂亮**优雅**。小燕的爸爸**指着**燕子窝对她说："看，妳是小燕子，它们也是小燕子，你们可以做**好朋友**呀。"

qù nián xià tiān, xiǎo yàn fā xiàn **mén kǒu** de **wū yán** xià yǒu yī gè yàn zǐ **wō**, **lín jū** men dōu shuō zhè xiàng zhēng zhe **jí lì**. yàn zǐ wō lǐ zhù zhe liǎng zhī xiǎo yàn zǐ, tā men hěn **kě ài**. hēi sè de **yǔ máo**, bái sè de **dù pí**, yī shuāng **líng huó** de xiǎo **yǎn jīng**, xiàng yī duì **hēi liàng** de **bǎo shí**, **jiǎn dāo** sì de **wěi bā**, hǎo xiàng shēn chuān yī jiàn **yàn wěi fú**, piāo liàng **yōu yǎ**. xiǎo yàn de bà ba **zhǐ zhe** yàn zǐ wō duì tā shuō: "kàn, nǐ shì xiǎo yàn zǐ, tā men yě shì xiǎo yàn zǐ, nǐ men kě yǐ zuò **hǎo péng yǒu** ya. "

小燕也很喜欢燕子们，她**查找**了许多关于燕子的**资料**。原来燕子是**秋去春来**的**候鸟**。北方的**冬天**寒冷，每年的**秋天**，燕子就会飞往**南方**过冬。等到**第二年**的**春天**再飞回来。**路途**很远，可是燕子却不会**迷失方向**，它总能找到去年的旧**巢**。燕子是**捕捉虫子**的**能手**，一窝燕子在一个夏天内能捕捉到几十万只**昆虫**。燕子喜欢把巢**安**在人家的屋檐下，它们用**嘴巴衔**来**泥土**、**草叶**和树枝，**筑**成一个**碗状**的小泥巢。然后两只燕子就住进去，并在泥巢里**产卵孵**小燕子。小燕总是在家门口发现几根羽毛，原来燕子经常把自己的羽毛留在某个地方，告诉别的燕子，这里是可以安全生活的地方。

xiǎo yàn yě hěn xǐ huān yàn zǐ men, tā **chá zhǎo** le xǔ duō guān yú yàn zǐ de **zī liào**. **yuán lái** yàn zǐ shì **qiū qù chūn lái** de **hòu niǎo**. běi fāng de **dōng tiān** hán lěng, měi nián de **qiū tiān**, yàn zǐ jiù hui fēi wǎng **nán fāng** guò dōng. děng dào **dì èr nián** de **chūn tiān** zài fēi huí lái. **lù tú** hěn yuǎn, kě shì yàn zǐ què bú huì **mí shī fāng xiàng**, tā zǒng néng zhǎo dào qù nián de jiù **cháo**. yàn zǐ shì **bǔ zhuō chóng zǐ** de **néng shǒu**, yī wō yàn zǐ zài yī gè xià tiān nèi néng bǔ zhuō dào jǐ shí wàn zhī **kūn chóng**. yàn zǐ xǐ huān bǎ cháo ān zài rén jiā de wū yán xià, tā men yòng **zuǐ bā xián** lái **ní tǔ, cǎo yè** hé shù zhī, **zhù** chéng yī gè **wǎn zhuàng** de xiǎo ní cháo. rán hòu liǎng zhī yàn zǐ jiù zhù jìn qù, bìng zài ní cháo lǐ **chǎn luǎn fū** xiǎo yàn zǐ. xiǎo yàn zǒng shì zài jiā mén kǒu fā xiàn jǐ gēn yǔ máo, yuán lái yàn zǐ jīng cháng bǎ zì jǐ de yǔ máo liú zài mǒu gè dì fāng, gào sù bié de yàn zǐ, zhè lǐ shì kě yǐ ān quán shēng huó de dì fāng.

小燕家屋檐下的两只小燕子每天从屋檐下**飞进飞出**，**唧唧喳喳**，**忙碌**又快乐。每天小燕出门的时候，燕子们会从屋檐下飞出来，**张开**翅膀飞在前面，好像是在陪她上学。当她放学回家的时候，它们就会在空中**盘旋**，**欢快**地叫着，**迎接**她回来。小燕和燕子之间好像有**说不出来的**感情。

xiǎo yàn jiā wū yán xià de liǎng zhī xiǎo yàn zǐ měi tiān cóng wū yán xià **fēi jìn fēi chū**, **jī jī zhā zhā**, **máng lù** yòu kuài lè. měi tiān xiǎo yàn chū mén de shí hòu, yàn zǐ men huì cóng wū yán xià fēi chū lái, **zhāng kāi** chì bǎng fēi zài qián miàn, hǎo xiàng shì zài péi tā shàng xué. dāng tā fàng xué huí jiā de shí hòu, tā men jiù huì zài kōng zhōng **pán xuán**, **huān kuài** dì jiào zhe, **yíng jiē** tā huí lái. xiǎo yàn hé yàn zǐ zhī jiān hǎo xiàng yǒu **shuō bú chū lái de** gǎn qíng.

十一月，天气**渐渐地**冷了，小燕子们也飞到南方过冬去了。小燕心里一直**惦记**着它们：它们南方的家在哪里？那么遥远的路，它们能飞得动吗？明年它们真的能飞回来吗？

shí yī yuè, tiān qì **jiàn jiàn dì** lěng le, xiǎo yàn zǐ men yě fēi dào nán fāng guò dōng qù le. xiǎo yàn xīn lǐ yī zhí **diàn jì** zhe tā men: tā men nán fāng de jiā zài nǎ lǐ? nà me yáo yuǎn de lù, tā men néng fēi dé dòng ma? míng nián tā men zhēn de néng fēi huí lái ma?

十二月底开始下起了**雪**，小燕在院子里**堆**了一个**雪人**。天气越来越冷，北风**呼啸**，寒冷**刺骨**。小燕站在窗前看着院子里的雪人，觉得很**冷清**。她想念燕子们**清脆**的歌声。

shí èr yuè dǐ kāi shǐ **xià** qǐ le **xuě**, xiǎo yàn zài yuàn zǐ lǐ **duī** le yī gè **xuě rén**. tiān qì yuè lái yuè lěng, běi fēng **hū xiào**, hán lěng **cì gǔ**.

xiǎo yàn zhàn zài chuāng qián kàn zhe yuàn zǐ lǐ de xuě rén, jué dé hěn **lěng qīng**. tā xiǎng niàn yàn zǐ men **qīng cuì** de gē shēng.

元旦过去了，春节过去了，到了三月，积雪渐渐融化，光秃秃的树枝也开始长出新芽。四月里的一天早上，春暖花开，阳光明媚。小燕早上睁开眼睛，似乎听到了叽叽喳喳的声音。她起床后打开门，站在门口抬头看，屋檐下燕子窝的主人果然回来了，正在对着她叫呢，好像是在说："好久不见，妳还好吗？"。

yuán dàn guò qù le, chūn jiē guò qù le, dào le sān yuè, **jī xuě** jiàn jiàn **róng huà**, **guāng tū tū** de shù zhī yě kāi shǐ zhǎng chū xīn **yá**. sì yuè lǐ de yī tiān zǎo shàng, **chūn nuǎn huā kāi**, yáng guāng **míng mèi**. xiǎo yàn zǎo shàng **zhēng kāi yǎn jīng**, sì hū tīng dào le jī jī zhā zhā de shēng yīn. tā qǐ chuáng hòu dǎ kāi mén, zhàn zài mén kǒu tái tóu kàn, wū yán xià yàn zǐ wō de **zhǔ rén** guǒ rán huí lái le, zhèng zài duì zhe tā jiào ne, hǎo xiàng shì zài shuō: "**hǎo jiǔ bú jiàn**, nǐ hái hǎo ma?".

小燕开心地笑了，她唱起了一首儿歌："小燕子，穿花衣，年年春天到这里。我问燕子为啥来？燕子说：这里的春天最美丽。"

xiǎo yàn kāi xīn dì xiào le, tā chàng qǐ le yī shǒu **ér gē**: "xiǎo yàn zǐ, chuān **huā yī**, nián nián chūn tiān dào zhè lǐ. wǒ wèn yàn zǐ **wéi shá** lái? yàn zǐ shuō: zhè lǐ de chūn tiān zuì měi lì. "

总结 （zǒng jié- Summary

去年夏天，小燕在屋檐下发现了一个燕子窝，里面住着两只燕子。她和燕子成为了朋友。在寒冷的冬天，燕子飞去南方过冬了，小燕很想念它们。第二年春天，两只燕子又飞回来了。

qù nián xià tiān, xiǎo yàn zài wū yán xià fā xiàn le yī gè yàn zǐ wō, lǐ miàn zhù zhe liǎng zhī yàn zǐ. tā hé yàn zǐ chéng wéi le péng yǒu. zài hán lěng de dōng tiān, yàn zǐ fēi qù nán fāng guò dōng le, xiǎo yàn hěn xiǎng niàn tā men. dì èr nián chūn tiān, liǎng zhī yàn zǐ yòu fēi huí lái le.

Summary of the story

Last summer, a girl named Xiao Yan (meaning little swallow in Chinese) found a swallow nest under the eaves of her home, with two swallows living inside. She became good friends with them. When the cold winter came, the swallows left for the south for the winter. Xiaoyan missed them. To her joy, the next spring, the two swallows came back to their old home under her eaves.

Vocabulary

- 名字 (míng zì): name
- 北方 (běi fāng): the north, the northern part of
- 城市 (chéng shì): city
- 燕子 (yàn zǐ): swallow (bird)
- 像 (xiàng): be like, looks like
- 飞来飞去 (fēi lái fēi qù): to fly over and away
- 活泼 (huó pō): full of life, lively
- 灵巧 (líng qiǎo): nimble, dexterous
- 长发 (cháng fā): long hair
- 扎 (zhā): to tie up, to bind
- 辫子 (biàn zǐ): braid, pigtail
- 翅膀 (chì bǎng): wing
- 去年 (qù nián): last year
- 夏天 (xià tiān): summer
- 门口 (mén kǒu): entrance, doorway
- 屋檐 (wū yán): eave
- 窝 (wō): nest, den
- 邻居 (lín jū): neighbor
- 吉利 (jí lì): auspicious
- 可爱 (kě ài): lovely, adorable
- 羽毛 (yǔ máo): feather, plume
- 肚皮 (dù pí): belly
- 灵活 (líng huó): agile, flexible
- 眼睛 (yǎn jīng): eye
- 黑亮 (hēi liàng): black and shiny
- 宝石 (bǎo shí): gemstone, precious stone
- 剪刀 (jiǎn dāo): scissors
- 尾巴 (wěi bā): tail
- 燕尾服 (yàn wěi fú): tail coat, swallow-tailed coat
- 优雅 (yōu yǎ): elegant
- 指着 (zhǐ zhe): to point at
- 好朋友 (hǎo péng yǒu): good friends
- 查找 (chá zhǎo): look up (about)
- 资料 (zī liào): information, materials

- 原来 (yuán lái): it turns out to be
- 秋去春来 (qiū qù chūn lái): going away in autumn, coming back in spring
- 侯鸟 (hòu niǎo): migratory bird
- 冬天 (dōng tiān): winter
- 秋天 (qiū tiān): autumn, fall
- 南方 (nán fāng): the south, the southern part of
- 第二年 (dì èr nián): the second year
- 春天 (chūn tiān): spring
- 路途 (lù tú): journey, path, way
- 迷失 (mí shī): to get lost
- 方向 (fāng xiàng): direction, orientation
- 巢 (cháo): nest
- 捕捉 (bǔ zhuō): catch, seize
- 虫子 (chóng zǐ): bug, worm
- 能手 (néng shǒu): dab, expert
- 昆虫 (kūn chóng): insect
- 嘴巴 (zuǐ bā): mouth
- 衔 (xián): to hold in the mouth
- 泥土 (ní tǔ): soil, earth
- 草叶 (cǎo yè): grass leaves
- 筑 (zhù): to build, to forge
- 碗状 (wǎn zhuàng): shaped like a bowl
- 产卵 (chǎn luǎn): lay eggs
- 孵 (fū): to sit on eggs, to hatch or incubate
- 飞进飞出 (fēi jìn fēi chū): to fly in and out
- 唧唧喳喳/叽叽喳喳 (jī jī zhā zhā): to chirp or twitter
- 忙碌 (máng lù): be busy
- 张开 (zhāng kāi): to open wide, to spread
- 盘旋 (pán xuán): to hover, to circle around
- 欢快 (huān kuài): cheerful, light-hearted
- 迎接 (yíng jiē): to welcome, to greet and meet upon someone's arrival

- 说不出来的 (**shuō bú chū lái de**): unspeakable, unutterable
- 渐渐地 (**jiàn jiàn dì**): gradually
- 惦记 (**diàn jì**): be concerned about, keep thinking about
- 下雪 (**xià xuě**): to snow
- 堆 (**duī**): to pile up
- 雪人 (**xuě rén**): snowman
- 呼啸 (**hū xiào**): to howl, to make a whistling sound
- 刺骨 (**cì gǔ**): a piercing, biting feeling
- 冷清 (**lěng qīng**): desolate, deserted
- 清脆 (**qīng cuì**): clear and melodious
- 元旦 (**yuán dàn**): New Year's day
- 积雪 (**jī xuě**): accumulated snow
- 融化 (**róng huà**): to melt, to thaw
- 光秃秃 (**guāng tū tū**): bald
- 芽 (**yá**): bud, sprout
- 春暖花开 (**chūn nuǎn huā kāi**): spring has come and all the flowers are in bloom
- 明媚 (**míng mèi**): radiant and enchanting
- 睁开眼睛 (**zhēng kāi yǎn jīng**): to open the eyes
- 主人 (**zhǔ rén**): owner, proprietor
- 好久不见 (**hǎo jiǔ bú jiàn**): It's been a long time since we last met, long time no see
- 儿歌 (**ér gē**): children's song, nursery rhymes
- 花衣 (**huā yī**): clothes with flower patterns or colorful patterns in general
- 为啥 (**wéi shá**): why

Questions about the story

1. 小燕家住在哪里？

   xiǎo yàn jiā zhù zài nǎ lǐ?

   a) 中国的北方

   zhōng guó de běi fāng

   b) 中国的南方

   zhōng guó de nán fāng

   c) 北京

   běi jīng

2. 下列说法中错误的是？

   xià liè shuō fǎ zhōng cuò wù de shì?

   a) 燕子象征着吉利

   yàn zi xiàng zhēng zhe jí lì

   b) 燕子已经在小燕家的屋檐下住了好多年

   yàn zi yǐ jīng zài xiǎo yàn jiā de wū yán xià zhù le hǎo duō

   nián

   c) 燕子和小燕是好朋友

   yàn zi hé xiǎo yàn shì hǎo péng yǒu

3. 关于燕子，哪种说法是正确的？

   guān yú yàn zi, nǎ zhǒng shuō fǎ shì zhèng què de?

   a) 燕子在春天飞到南方，冬天飞回北方

   yàn zi zài chūn tiān fēi dào nán fāng, dōng tiān fēi huí běi

   fāng

b) 燕子喜欢把巢筑在树上

yàn zi xǐ huān bǎ cháo zhù zài shù shàng

c) 燕子捕捉昆虫

yàn zi bǔ zhuō kūn chóng

4. 冬天下雪的时候：

dōng tiān xià xuě de shí hòu:

a) 燕子和小燕一起堆了一个雪人

yàn zi hé xiǎo yàn yī qǐ duī le yī gè xuě rén

b) 小燕在院子里堆了一个雪人

xiǎo yàn zài yuan zi lǐ duī le yī gè xuě rén

c) 小燕去了南方

xiǎo yàn qù le nán fāng

5. 燕子是什么时候飞回来的？

yàn zi shì shén me shí hòu fēi huí lái de?

a) 三月

sān yuè

b) 夏天

xià tiān

c) 四月

sì yuè

Answers

1. B
2. A
3. B
4. C
5. C

Chapter VII

丢钱包 (DIŪ QIÁN BĀO)

星期一的早上，严飞**急匆匆**地跑出家门，骑上**电动摩托车**，用比往常更快的速度向**公司驶**去。他前一天晚上看**球赛**到**凌晨**三点，今天早上七点半的闹钟响了，可是他八点半才**醒来**，于是**早饭**也没吃就赶去**上班**了。还好，路上没有遇到**红灯**，九点还差两分钟的时候进了公司，严飞感到十分**庆幸**。星期一上午公司总是很忙，他**来不及**多想就立即开始工作了。

xīng qī yī de zǎo shàng, yán fēi **jí cōng cōng** dì pǎo chū jiā mén, qí shàng **diàn dòng mó tuō chē**, yòng bǐ wǎng cháng gèng kuài de sù dù xiàng **gōng sī shǐ** qù. tā qián yī tiān wǎn shàng kàn **qiú sài** dào **líng chén** sān diǎn, jīn tiān zǎo shàng qī diǎn bàn de nào zhōng xiǎng le, kě shì tā bā diǎn bàn cái **xǐng lái**, yú shì **zǎo fàn** yě méi chī jiù gǎn qù **shàng bān** le. hái hǎo, lù shàng méi yǒu yù dào **hóng dēng**, jiǔ diǎn hái chà liǎng fèn zhōng de shí hòu jìn le gōng sī, yán fēi gǎn dào shí fèn **qìng xìng**. xīng qī yī **shàng wǔ** gōng sī zǒng shì hěn máng, tā **lái bú jí** duō xiǎng jiù **lì jí** kāi shǐ gōng zuò le.

不知不觉就到了**中午**，因为没吃早饭，严飞早就**饿**了。他把上午的工作**整理**好，**准备去吃午饭**。**同事**王凯过来，对他说："严飞，公司**楼下**有一家**新开的餐馆**，听说味道不错，我们去**尝尝**吧。"严飞回答道："好啊，我可真饿了，等我拿了钱包就跟你去。"他的钱包通常放在**公文包外侧**的**口袋**里，可是当他打开口袋，却没有找到。他把公文包从里到外都检查了一遍，还是没有。他**紧张**了起来，把衣服口袋和**办公桌**都找了一遍，**依然**没有钱包。

bú zhī bú jué jiù dào le **zhōng wǔ**, yīn wéi méi chī zǎo fàn, yán fēi zǎo jiù **è** le. tā bǎ shàng wǔ de gōng zuò **zhěng lǐ** hǎo, **zhǔn bèi** qù chī **wǔ fàn**. **tóng shì** wáng kǎi guò lái, duì tā shuō: "yán fēi, gōng sī **lóu xià** yǒu yī jiā **xīn kāi de cān guǎn**, **tīng shuō wèi dào** bú cuò, wǒ men qù **cháng cháng** ba. "yán fēi huí dá **dào**: "hǎo ā, wǒ kě zhēn è le, děng wǒ ná le qián bāo jiù gēn nǐ qù. "tā de qián bāo tōng cháng fàng zài **gōng wén bāo wài cè** de **kǒu dài** lǐ, kě shì dāng tā dǎ kāi kǒu dài, què méi yǒu zhǎo dào. tā bǎ gōng wén bāo cóng lǐ dào wài dōu jiǎn chá le yī biàn, hái shì méi yǒu. tā **jǐn zhāng** le qǐ lái, bǎ yī fú kǒu dài hé **bàn gōng zhuō** dōu zhǎo le yī biàn, **yī rán** méi yǒu qián bāo.

王凯见他**焦急**的样子，问："**怎么了？**"严飞说："我的钱包好像**丢了**。"王凯**惊讶**道："**真的吗**？在哪儿丢的呢？"严飞**皱**着眉头说："我也不知道。我早上从家里出来，就**直接**来公司了，早饭都没吃。"他指了指公文包："平常钱包都放在那里，可是现在找不到了。"王凯拿起公文包**仔细**看了看，**叫道**："**哎呀**，你的包**拉链坏了**！"严飞把包拿过来一看，**可不是吗**，平常放钱包的口袋拉链不知道什么时候坏了，**即使**拉起来，口袋还是**敞开**的。他想：钱包一定是在自己骑电动车**赶路**的时候从包里**掉出**来了。一路上那么多的人和车，也不知道是在哪里掉出来的。又经过了一个上午，钱包**肯定**找不到了。

wáng kǎi jiàn tā **jiāo jí** de yàng zǐ, wèn: "**zěn me le**? "yán fēi shuō: "wǒ de qián bāo hǎo xiàng **diū le**. "wáng kǎi **jīng yà** dào: "**zhēn de ma**? zài nǎ ér diū de ne? "yán fēi **zhòu** zhe **méi tóu** shuō: "wǒ yě bú zhī dào. wǒ zǎo shàng cóng jiā lǐ chū lái, jiù **zhí jiē** lái gōng sī le,

zǎo fàn dōu méi chī. "tā zhǐ le zhǐ gōng wén bāo: "píng cháng qián
bāo dōu fàng zài nà lǐ, kě shì xiàn zài zhǎo bú dào le. "wáng kǎi ná
qǐ gōng wén bāo **zǐ xì** kàn le kàn, **jiào** dào: "**āi ya**, nǐ de bāo **lā liàn
huài le!** "yán fēi bǎ bāo ná guò lái yī kàn, **kě bú shì ma**, píng cháng
fàng qián bāo de kǒu dài lā liàn bú zhī dào shí me shí hòu huài le, **jí
shǐ** lā qǐ lái, kǒu dài hái shì **chǎng kāi** de. tā xiǎng: qián bāo yī dìng
shì zài zì jǐ qí diàn dòng chē **gǎn lù** de shí hòu cóng bāo lǐ **diào chū**
lái le. yī lù shàng nà me duō de rén hé chē, yě bú zhī dào shì zài nǎ
lǐ diào chū lái de. yòu jīng guò le yī gè shàng wǔ, qián bāo **kěn dìng**
zhǎo bú dào le.

严飞又**沮丧**又**担心**，因为钱包里除了**现金**，还有他的几张银行
卡，**如果**真的丢了就**麻烦**了。他无力地坐在椅子上，王凯**拍拍**
他的**肩膀**说："别难过了，我**请客**，先去吃饭，别饿着肚子。**就
算**钱包真的丢了，也要**吃饱**了再来**处理**。"严飞无奈地叹了口气，
跟着王凯去了楼下新开的餐馆。

yán fēi yòu **jǔ sàng** yòu **dān xīn**, yīn wéi qián bāo lǐ chú le **xiàn jīn**,
hái yǒu tā de jǐ zhāng yín háng kǎ, **rú guǒ** zhēn de diū le jiù **má fán**
le. tā **wú lì** dì zuò zài yǐ zǐ shàng, wáng kǎi **pāi pāi** tā de **jiān bǎng**
shuō: "bié **nán guò** le, wǒ **qǐng kè**, xiān qù chī fàn, bié è zhe dù zǐ.
jiù suàn qián bāo zhēn de diū le, yě yào **chī bǎo** le zài lái
chǔ lǐ. "yán fēi **wú nài** dì **tàn le kǒu qì**, gēn zhe wáng kǎi qù le lóu
xià xīn kāi de cān guǎn.

严飞想着钱包的事情，**心不在焉**地吃着饭，**突然**手机响了。他
接了电话，听到一个**陌生**的声音问："**请问**是严先生吗？"严飞
答道："我就是。"对方说："您是不是丢了钱包？"严飞**惊喜**道：
"对呀，您怎么知道？"对方说："**太好了**！我早上在路上**捡**到了
一个钱包，里面有**名片**，就按照名片上的电话号码打给您了。

请您**有空**来取吧。"严飞**激动地**说："**太感谢了**！您的**地址**是哪里呢？""人民路111号，春风餐馆，我是餐馆的**老板**。"

yán fēi xiǎng zhe qián bāo de shì qíng, **xīn bú zài yān** dì chī zhe fàn, **tū rán** shǒu jī xiǎng le. tā jiē le diàn huà, tīng dào yī gè **mò shēng** de shēng yīn wèn: "**qǐng wèn** shì yán xiān shēng ma?" yán fēi dá dào: "wǒ jiù shì. "duì fāng shuō: "nín shì bú shì diū le qián bāo?" yán fēi **jīng xǐ** dào: "duì ya, nín zěn me zhī dào?" duì fāng shuō: "**tài hǎo le**! wǒ zǎo shàng zài lù shàng **jiǎn dào** le yī gè qián bāo, lǐ miàn yǒu **míng piàn**, jiù àn zhào míng piàn shàng de diàn huà hào mǎ dǎ gěi nín le. qǐng nín **yǒu kòng** lái qǔ ba." yán fēi **jī dòng** dì shuō: "**tài gǎn xiè le**! nín de **dì zhǐ** shì nǎ lǐ ne" "rén mín lù 111 hào, chūn fēng cān guǎn, wǒ shì cān guǎn de **lǎo bǎn**. "

"人民路？那不就是这里吗"，严飞**自言自语**："春风餐馆？好像在哪里听说过……"王凯说："这家餐馆就叫春风餐馆呀！"严飞**抬头望向**柜台，老板拿着手机，也正在惊讶地看着他呢！

"rén mín lù? nà bú jiù shì zhè lǐ ma ", yán fēi **zì yán zì yǔ**: "chūn fēng cān guǎn? hǎo xiàng zài nǎ lǐ tīng shuō guò……"wáng kǎi shuō: "zhè jiā cān guǎn jiù jiào chūn fēng cān guǎn ya! "yán fēi **tái tóu wàng xiàng** guì tái, lǎo bǎn ná zhe shǒu jī, yě zhèng zài jīng yà dì kàn zhe tā ne!

总结 （zǒng jié- Summary

严飞的公文包拉链坏了，放在里面的钱包在上班路上丢了。正在他焦急之时，吃午饭的餐馆老板打来电话，原来他的钱包就是被这位老板捡到了，这让严飞十分惊喜。

yán fēi de gōng wén bāo lā liàn huài le, fàng zài lǐ miàn de qián bāo zài shàng bān lù shàng diū le. zhèng zài tā jiāo jí zhī shí, chī wǔ fàn de cān guǎn lǎo bǎn dǎ lái diàn huà, yuán lái tā de qián bāo jiù shì bèi zhè wèi lǎo bǎn jiǎn dào le, zhè ràng yán fēi shí fèn jīng xǐ.

Summary of the story

Due to a broken zipper on his portfolio case, Yan Fei's wallet dropped out on his way to work and got lost. While he was anxious and worried about this, the boss of the restaurant where he was having lunch called him. It turns out the restaurant boss has found his wallet. It was a great surprise.

Vocabulary

- **急匆匆 (jí cōng cōng):** in a hurry
- **电动 (diàn dòng):** electric
- **摩托车 (mó tuō chē):** motorcycle
- **公司 (gōng sī):** company
- **驶 (shǐ):** to drive, to ride
- **球赛 (qiú sài):** football game
- **凌晨 (líng chén):** midnight
- **醒来 (xǐng lái):** to wake up
- **早饭 (zǎo fàn):** breakfast
- **上班 (shàng bān):** to go to work
- **红灯 (hóng dēng):** red (traffic) light
- **庆幸 (qìng xìng):** to feel lucky about
- **上午 (shàng wǔ):** morning, before noon
- **来不及 (lái bú jí):** not enough time to do something
- **立即 (lì jí):** immediately
- **不知不觉 (bú zhī bú jué):** unconsciously, unknowingly
- **中午 (zhōng wǔ):** noon
- **饿 (è):** be hungry
- **整理 (zhěng lǐ):** to put in order, to clean up
- **准备 (zhǔn bèi):** be prepared, be ready
- **午饭 (wǔ fàn):** lunch
- **同事 (tóng shì):** colleague, coworker
- **楼下 (lóu xià):** downstairs
- **新开的 (xīn kāi de):** newly or recently opened
- **餐馆 (cān guǎn):** restaurant
- **听说 (tīng shuō):** hear of, hear about
- **味道 (wèi dào):** taste, flavor
- **尝尝 (cháng cháng):** to have a taste of something
- **道 (dào):** to say

- 公文包 (gōng wén bāo): portfolio case, portfolio bag
- 外侧 (wài cè): external, outside
- 口袋 (kǒu dài): pocket
- 紧张 (jǐn zhāng): be nervous
- 办公桌 (bàn gōng zhuō): office desk
- 依然 (yī rán): to remain, still
- 焦急 (jiāo jí): be anxious, worried
- 怎么了 (zěn me le): What's wrong? What happened?
- 丢了 (diū le): to get lost
- 惊讶 (jīng yà): be surprised
- 真的吗 (zhēn de ma): Really? Is it true?
- 皱眉头 (zhòu méi tóu): to frown
- 直接 (zhí jiē): directly
- 仔细 (zǐ xì): carefully
- 叫 (jiào): to yell, to shout
- 哎呀 (āi ya): Ah! Ouch!
- 拉链 (lā liàn): zipper
- 坏了 (huài le): be broken, malfunctional
- 可不是吗 (kě bú shì ma): Isn't it?
- 即使 (jí shǐ): even if
- 敞开 (chǎng kāi): be widely open
- 赶路 (gǎn lù): to hurry on with one's journey
- 掉出 (diào chū): to drop out
- 肯定 (kěn dìng): definitely, for sure
- 沮丧 (jǔ sàng): be depressed, to feel down
- 担心 (dān xīn): to worry, be worried
- 现金 (xiàn jīn): cash
- 如果 (rú guǒ): if
- 麻烦 (má fán): be troublesome, to bring troubles

- **无力 (wú lì):** be lack of energy
- **拍拍 (pāi pāi):** to pat on
- **肩膀 (jiān bǎng):** shoulder
- **难过 (nán guò):** be sad
- **请客 (qǐng kè):** to treat someone to something (a meal)
- **就算 (jiù suàn):** even if
- **吃饱 (chī bǎo):** to eat until full
- **处理 (chǔ lǐ):** to handle, to deal with
- **无奈 (wú nài):** to have no choice but
- **叹了口气 (tàn le kǒu qì):** to let out a sigh
- **心不在焉 (xīn bú zài yān):** be absent-minded
- **突然 (tū rán):** suddenly
- **陌生 (mò shēng):** strange, unfamiliar
- **请问 (qǐng wèn):** excuse me, may I ask
- **惊喜 (jīng xǐ):** be pleasantly surprised
- **太好了 (tài hǎo le):** that's great, great
- **捡到 (jiǎn dào):** to pick up, to find
- **名片 (míng piàn):** namecard, business card
- **有空 (yǒu kòng):** be free, available, have time
- **激动 (jī dòng):** be excited
- **太感谢了 (tài gǎn xiè le):** thank you so much
- **地址 (dì zhǐ):** address
- **老板 (lǎo bǎn):** boss, owner
- **自言自语 (zì yán zì yǔ):** to talk to oneself
- **抬头 (tái tóu):** to raise one's head
- **望向 (wàng xiàng):** to look towards

Questions about the story

1. 严飞早上为什么急匆匆的？

   yán fēi zǎo shang wèi shé me jí cōng cōng de?

   a) 因为他忘记开闹钟了

   yīn wèi tā wàng jì kāi nào zhōng le

   b) 因为他忘记带钱包了

   yīn wèi tā wàng jì dài qián bāo le

   c) 因为他前一天晚上看球赛而很晚睡

   yīn wèi tā qián yī tiān wǎn shàng kàn qiú sài ér hěn wǎn shuì

2. 严飞上班的交通工具是：

   yán fēi shàng bān de jiāo tōng gōng jù shì:

   a) 电动摩托车

   diàn dòng mó tuō chē

   b) 公交车

   gōng jiāo chē

   c) 自行车

   zì xíng chē

3. 严飞是什么时候发现钱包丢了的？

   yán fēi shì shén me shí hòu fā xiàn qián bāo diū le de?

   a) 一到公司就发现了

   yī dào gōng sī jiù fā xiàn le

   b) 中午吃午饭前

   zhōng wǔ chī wǔ fàn qián

c) 到餐馆以后

dào cān guǎn yǐ hòu

4. 下列正确的说法是：

xià liè zhèng què de shuō fǎ shì:

a) 是严飞先发现自己的公文包拉链坏了

shì yán fēi xiān fā xiàn zì jǐ de gōng wén bāo lā liàn huài le

b) 王凯把严飞公文包的拉链弄坏了

wáng kǎi bǎ yán fēi gōng wén bāo de lā liàn nòng huài le

c) 严飞早上没有发现包的拉链坏了

yán fēi zǎo shang méi yǒu fā xiàn bāo de lā liàn huài le

5. 从故事的结尾推断，以下不正确的是：

cóng gù shì de jié wěi tuī duàn, yǐ xià bù zhèng què de shì:

a) 餐馆老板也发现了严飞就是和他打电话的人

cān guǎn lǎo bǎn yě fā xiàn le yán fēi jiù shì hé tā dǎ diàn

huà de rén

b) 严飞和餐馆老板以前就认识

yán fēi hé cān guǎn lǎo bǎn yǐ qián jiù rèn shì

c) 餐馆老板也感到很惊讶

cān guǎn lǎo bǎn yě gǎn dào hěn jīng yà

Answers

1. C
2. A
3. B
4. C
5. B

Chapter VIII

谁偷吃了芒果？
(SHUÍ TŌU CHĪ LE MÁNG GUǑ?)

在**泰国**的一个**村庄**里，有一座**花园**，花园里种着一棵**芒果树**。花园的主人是一位**老爷爷**，他一直**用心照顾**这棵芒果树，从它还是绿色的小苗开始，为它**浇水、施肥、除虫**。五年过去了，小**树苗**长成了大树，但是还从来没有**结果**。老爷爷并不着急，一直耐心地等待，他相信有一天，这棵树一定会结出又大又甜的芒果。

zài **tài guó** de yī gè **cūn zhuāng** lǐ, yǒu yī zuò **huā yuán**, huā yuán lǐ zhǒng zhe yī kē máng guǒ shù. huā yuán de zhǔ rén shì yī wèi **lǎo yé yé**, tā yī zhí **yòng xīn zhào gù** zhè kē máng guǒ shù, cóng tā hái shì lǜ sè de xiǎo miáo kāi shǐ, wéi tā **jiāo shuǐ, shī féi, chú chóng**. wǔ nián guò qù le, xiǎo **shù miáo** zhǎng chéng le dà shù, dàn shì hái cóng lái méi yǒu **jié guǒ**. lǎo yé yé bìng bú zhe jí, yī zhí nài xīn dì děng dài, tā xiàng xìn yǒu yī tiān, zhè kē shù yī dìng huì jié chū yòu dà yòu tián de máng guǒ.

这一年的二月，老爷爷惊喜地发现，芒果树**开花**了！在长长的**深绿色**叶子之间，**淡黄色**的小花开放着，虽然每朵花只有**手指**尖那么小，但许多小花**密集地聚**在一起，远远看去就像是一团团淡黄色的**雾**。虽然花小，它们**散发**出来的香气可是相当**浓郁**，香甜的气息把蜜蜂吸引过来在花间飞舞。老爷爷高兴极了，他更加细心照顾芒果树，期待着夏天的果实。

zhè yī nián de èr yuè, lǎo yé yé jīng xǐ dì fā xiàn, máng guǒ shù **kāi huā** le! zài cháng cháng de **shēn lǜ sè** yè zǐ zhī jiān, **dàn huáng sè** de xiǎo huā kāi fàng zhe, suī rán měi duǒ huā zhī yǒu **shǒu zhǐ jiān** nà me xiǎo, dàn xǔ duō xiǎo huā **mì jí dì jù** zài yī qǐ, yuǎn yuǎn kàn qù jiù xiàng shì yī tuán tuán dàn huáng sè de **wù**. suīrán huā xiǎo, tā men **sàn fā** chū lái de **xiāng qì** kě shì xiàng dāng **nóng yù, xiāng tián** de **qì xī** bǎ **mì fēng** xī yǐn guò lái zài huā jiān **fēi wǔ**. lǎo yé yé gāo xìng jí le, tā gèng jiā xì xīn zhào gù máng guǒ shù, **qī dài** zhe xià tiān de **guǒ shí**.

五月，芒果树的枝头开始长出小小的果实。一开始只有葡萄那么大，慢慢变成鸡蛋那么大，再到一个人的拳头那么大……颜色也从青绿色逐渐变黄。果实一开始又小又硬，随着长大和颜色变黄，也开始变得柔软了，从树枝上垂下来，散发出芒果的芳香。老爷爷每天早上和晚上都要数一遍树上结了多少个芒果，数字一天天增加，每天数芒果的时候也成了他最快乐的时候。他特别注意几个快要成熟的最大的芒果，心里想着：等它们成熟了，我要先尝一尝，然后就把邻居们都请到花园里来，让他们也吃到这美味的芒果。

wǔ yuè, máng guǒ shù de **zhī tóu** kāi shǐ zhǎng chū xiǎo xiǎo de guǒ shí. **yī kāi shǐ** zhī yǒu **pú táo** nà me dà, màn màn biàn chéng **jī dàn** nà me dà, zài dào yī gè rén de **quán tóu** nà me dà……yán sè yě cóng **qīng lǜ sè** zhú jiàn biàn huáng. guǒ shí yī kāi shǐ yòu xiǎo yòu **yìng**, suí zhe zhǎng dà hé yán sè biàn huáng, yě kāi shǐ biàn dé **róu ruǎn** le, cóng shù zhī shàng **chuí xià** lái, sàn fā chū máng guǒ de **fāng xiāng**. lǎo yé yé měi tiān zǎo shàng hé wǎn shàng dōu yào **shǔ** yī biàn shù shàng jié le duō shǎo gè máng guǒ, shù zì yī tiān tiān zēng jiā, měi tiān shù máng guǒ de shí hòu yě chéng le tā zuì kuài lè de shí hòu. tā tè bié zhù yì jǐ gè kuài yào **chéng shú** de zuì dà de máng guǒ, xīn lǐ xiǎng zhe: děng tā men chéng shú le, wǒ yào xiān cháng yī cháng, rán hòu jiù bǎ lín jū men dōu qǐng dào huā yuán lǐ lái, ràng tā men yě chī dào zhè **měi wèi** de máng guǒ.

这天早上，老爷爷**满心期待**地来到花园里，前一天他看到最大的一个芒果已经成熟，今天可以**采摘**了。但是当他来到树下，却找不到那个大芒果了。他感到奇怪，于是把树上的果实全数了一遍，**不由得**惊叫道："怎么只有27个了，昨天还有28个的呢？"他**怀疑**自己数错了，又数了两遍，的确是27个。他又**低头**在树下的**草丛**里仔细寻找，也**一无所获**，看来最大的那个芒果不见了。老爷爷觉得又伤心又**困惑**，还有点儿生气：期待落空了，**到底**是谁**抢**在我前面把第一个芒果摘了？

zhè tiān zǎo shàng, lǎo yé yé **mǎn xīn qī dài** dì lái dào huā yuán lǐ, qián yī tiān tā kàn dào zuì dà de yī gè máng guǒ yǐ jīng chéng shú, jīn tiān kě yǐ **cǎi zhāi** le. dàn shì dāng tā lái dào shù xià, què zhǎo bú dào nà gè dà máng guǒ le. tā gǎn dào qí guài, yú shì bǎ shù shàng de guǒ shí quán shù le yī biàn, **bú yóu dé** jīng jiào dào: "zěn me zhǐ yǒu 27 gè le, zuó tiān hái yǒu 28 gè de ne?" tā **huái yí** zì jǐ shù cuò le, yòu shù le liǎng biàn, dí què shì 27 gè. tā yòu **dī tóu** zài shù xià de **cǎo cóng** lǐ zī xì xún zhǎo, yě **yī wú suǒ huò**, kàn lái zuì dà de nà gè máng guǒ bú jiàn le. lǎo yé yé jué dé yòu shāng xīn yòu **kùn huò**, hái yǒu diǎn ér shēng qì: qī dài luò kōng le, **dào dǐ** shì shuí **qiǎng** zài wǒ qián miàn bǎ dì yī gè máng guǒ zhāi le?

第二天早上，老爷爷像**往常**一样来数芒果，他发现，**竟然**又少了一个，只剩26个了！这次**失踪**的也是一个快要成熟的芒果。他**抚摸**着芒果树的树干说："到底是谁**偷吃**了你的果子？"但芒果树只是**随风摇摆**着树叶，**不发一言**。

dì èr tiān zǎo shàng, lǎo yé yé xiàng **wǎng cháng** yī yàng lái shù máng guǒ, tā fā xiàn, **jìng rán** yòu shǎo le yī gè, zhī shèng 26 gè le! zhè cì **shī zōng** de yě shì yī gè kuài yào chéng shú de máng guǒ. tā **fǔ mō** zhe máng guǒ shù de shù gàn shuō: "dào dǐ shì shuí **tōu chī** le nǐ de guǒ zǐ? "dàn máng guǒ shù zhī shì **suí fēng yáo bǎi** zhe shù yè, **bú fā yī yán**.

第三天早上，又少了一个。**这下老爷爷生气了：这个贼太可恶了！他决心要抓住这个偷吃芒果的家伙。太阳下山的时候还有25个芒果，于是他回到屋子里，从窗户盯着花园里的芒果树。夜深了，但月亮银色的光让他依然能看清花园里的一切。渐渐地，老爷爷觉得困倦，睁不开眼睛，坐在椅子上睡着了。**

dì sān tiān zǎo shàng, yòu shǎo le yī gè. **zhè xià** lǎo yé yé shēng qì le: zhè gè **zéi** tài **kě wù** le! tā jué xīn yào **zhuā zhù** zhè gè tōu chī máng guǒ de **jiā huǒ**. **tài yáng xià shān** de shí hòu hái yǒu 25 gè máng guǒ, yú shì tā huí dào wū zǐ lǐ, cóng chuāng hù **dīng zhe** huā yuán lǐ de máng guǒ shù. **yè shēn** le, dàn yuè liàng **yín sè** de guāng ràng tā yī rán néng kàn qīng huā yuán lǐ de **yī qiē**. **jiàn jiàn dì**, lǎo yé yé jué dé **kùn juàn**, zhēng bú kāi yǎn jīng, zuò zài yǐ zǐ shàng **shuì zháo** le.

不知道睡了多久，他被一阵"吱吱"的声音**惊醒**了。抬头一看，只见一个**黑影**正顺着芒果树的树干向上爬。老爷爷轻轻地走到窗前一看，原来是一只**猴子**。他从窗口朝花园里**扔**了一块小石头，把猴子**吓跑**了。

bú zhī dào shuì le duō jiǔ, tā bèi yī zhèn"**zhī zhī**"de shēng yīn **jīng xǐng** le. tái tóu yī kàn, zhī jiàn yī gè **hēi yǐng** zhèng **shùn zhe** máng guǒ shù de shù gàn xiàng shàng pá. lǎo yé yé qīng qīng dì zǒu dào chuāng qián yī kàn, yuán lái shì yī zhī **hóu zǐ**. tā cóng chuāng kǒu cháo huā yuán lǐ **rēng** le yī kuài xiǎo shí tóu, bǎ hóu zǐ **xià pǎo** le.

从第二天开始，老爷爷每天晚上都会在树下放几个**香蕉**，猴子吃了香蕉，就**满足**地走了。**剩**下的芒果就再也没有被偷吃过，老爷爷和邻居们一起**庆祝**了芒果大**丰收**。

còng dì èr tiān kāi shǐ, lǎo yé yé měi tiān wǎn shàng dōu huì zài shù xià fàng jǐ gè **xiāng jiāo**, hóu zǐ chī le xiāng jiāo, jiù **mǎn zú** dì zǒu le. **shèng xià** de máng guǒ jiù zài yě méi yǒu bèi tōu chī guò, lǎo yé yé hé lín jū men yī qǐ **qìng zhù** le máng guǒ dà **fēng shōu**.

总结 (zǒng jié- Summary

一位老爷爷在花园里种了一株芒果树。五年后，芒果树终于开花结果了，但果实却一连三天被偷。老爷爷发现偷吃芒果的贼原来是一只猴子，于是就用香蕉把猴子喂饱，迎来了芒果的丰收。

yī wèi lǎo yé yé zài huā yuán lǐ zhǒng le yī zhū máng guǒ shù. wǔ nián hòu, máng guǒ shù zhōng yú kāi huā jié guǒ le, dàn guǒ shí què yī lián sān tiān bèi tōu. lǎo yé yé fā xiàn tōu chī máng guǒ de zéi yuán lái shì yī zhī hóu zǐ, yú shì jiù yòng xiāng jiāo bǎ hóu zǐ wèi bǎo, yíng lái le máng guǒ de fēng shōu.

Summary of the story

An old man planted a mango tree in his garden. After five years of tender care, the tree finally went into blossom and then bore fruits. But for three days in a row, someone stole mangoes from the tree. The old man found that the mango thief was a monkey. He fed the monkey with bananas, and eventually secured a great mango harvest.

Vocabulary

- 泰国 **(tài guó)**: Thailand
- 村庄 **(cūn zhuāng)**: village
- 花园 **(huā yuán)**: garden
- 老爷爷 **(lǎo yé yé)**: old man
- 用心 **(yòng xīn)**: attentively, with care
- 照顾 **(zhào gù)**: to take care of
- 浇水 **(jiāo shuǐ)**: to water
- 施肥 **(shī féi)**: to apply fertilizer
- 除虫 **(chú chóng)**: to kill bugs, insects
- 树苗 **(shù miáo)**: sapling
- 结果 **(jié guǒ)**: to bear fruits
- 开花 **(kāi huā)**: to blossom
- 深绿色 **(shēn lǜ sè)**: deep green
- 淡黄色 **(dàn huáng sè)**: light yellow
- 手指尖 **(shǒu zhǐ jiān)**: finger tip
- 密集地 **(mì jí dì)**: concentrated, crowded
- 聚 **(jù)**: to gather
- 雾 **(wù)**: fog, mist
- 散发 **(sàn fā)**: to send out, to emanate
- 香气 **(xiāng qì)**: fragrance, aroma
- 浓郁 **(nóng yù)**: rich, strong
- 香甜 **(xiāng tián)**: sweet and fragrant
- 气息 **(qì xī)**: smell, flavor
- 蜜蜂 **(mì fēng)**: bee
- 飞舞 **(fēi wǔ)**: to dance in the air, to flutter
- 期待 **(qī dài)**: to expect, to look forward to
- 果实 **(guǒ shí)**: fruit
- 枝头 **(zhī tóu)**: on the branch
- 一开始 **(yī kāi shǐ)**: at the beginning
- 葡萄 **(pú táo)**: grape

- 鸡蛋 (jī dàn): egg
- 拳头 (quán tóu): fist
- 青绿色 (qīng lǜ sè): cyan, dark green
- 硬 (yìng): hard, tough
- 柔软 (róu ruǎn): soft, flexible
- 垂下 (chuí xià): to hang down
- 芳香 (fāng xiāng): sweet fragrance
- 数 (shǔ): to count
- 成熟 (chéng shú): (to become) mature, ripe
- 美味 (měi wèi): delicious, tasty
- 满心期待 (mǎn xīn qī dài): full of expectation
- 采摘 (cǎi zhāi): to pick
- 不由得 (bú yóu dé): cannot help but
- 怀疑 (huái yí): to doubt, to suspect
- 低头 (dī tóu): to lower one's head
- 草丛 (cǎo cóng): thick growth of grass, bush
- 一无所获 (yī wú suǒ huò): have gained nothing, empty-handed
- 困惑 (kùn huò): puzzled, confused
- 到底 (dào dǐ): in the end, after all
- 抢 (qiǎng): to beat someone to it
- 往常 (wǎng cháng): usual
- 竟然 (jìng rán): actually, to one's surprise
- 失踪 (shī zōng): to disappear, to go missing
- 抚摸 (fǔ mō): to caress, to fondle
- 偷吃 (tōu chī): to take food on the sly, to steal food
- 随风摇摆 (suí fēng yáo bǎi): to swing in the wind
- 不发一言 (bú fā yī yán): to keep silent, to say no word

- 这下 (zhè xià): this time
- 贼 (zéi): thief
- 可恶 (kě wù): detestable, abominable
- 抓住 (zhuā zhù): seize, capture
- 家伙 (jiā huǒ): guy, chap, fellow
- 太阳下山 (tài yáng xià shān): the sun sets
- 盯着 (dīng zhe): to stare at
- 夜深 (yè shēn): in the dead of night
- 银色 (yín sè): silver
- 一切 (yī qiē): everything, all
- 渐渐地 (jiàn jiàn dì): grandually
- 困倦 (kùn juàn): sleepy, drowsy
- 睡着 (shuì zháo): to fall asleep
- 吱吱 (zhī zhī): squeaking sounds
- 惊醒 (jīng xǐng): to wake up with a start
- 黑影 (hēi yǐng): silhouette
- 顺着 (shùn zhe): along
- 猴子 (hóu zǐ): monkey
- 扔 (rēng): to throw
- 吓跑 (xià pǎo): to scare off, to scare away
- 香蕉 (xiāng jiāo): banana
- 满足 (mǎn zú): be satisfied, be content
- 剩下 (shèng xià): the remaining
- 庆祝 (qìng zhù): to celebrate
- 丰收 (fēng shōu): harvest

Questions about the story

1. 老爷爷的芒果树

   lǎo yé yé de máng guǒ shù

   a) 每年都结果

   měi nián dōu jié guǒ

   b) 是五年前种下的

   shì wǔ nián qián zhǒng xià de

   c) 不会结果

   bù huì jié guǒ

2. 芒果的花是什么颜色？

   máng guǒ de huā shì shén me yán sè?

   a) 白色

   bái sè

   b) 淡黄色

   dàn huáng sè

   c) 绿色

   lǜ sè

3. 在没被偷吃前,一共有多少个芒果？

   zài méi bèi tōu chī qián, yī gòng yǒu duō shǎo gè máng guǒ?

   a) 25个

   25 gè

   b) 26个

   26 gè

c) 28个

   28 gè

4. 老爷爷是怎么发现偷芒果的贼？

   lǎo yé yé shì zěn me fā xiàn tōu máng guǒ de zéi?

   a) 在树下等着

      zài shù xià děng zhe

   b) 请邻居帮忙

      qǐng lín jū bang máng

   c) 在屋里盯着

      zài wū li ding zhe

5. 下列正确的说法是？

   xià liè zhèng què de shuō fǎ shì?

   a) 猴子喜欢吃香蕉

      hóu zi xǐ huān chī xiāng jiāo

   b) 芒果的花有香味，果实没有

      máng guǒ de huā yǒu xiāng wèi, guǒ shí méi yǒu

   c) 老爷爷把猴子抓住了

      lǎo yé yé bǎ hóu zi zhuā zhù le

Answers

1. B
2. B
3. C
4. C
5. A

Chapter IX

刻舟求剑 (KÈ ZHŌU QIÚ JIÀN)

古代的中国**分成**很多个小国家，其中有一个国家叫**楚国**。在楚国的一处有一条**江**，江面宽阔，江水湍急，必须**乘船**才能**往返**于江的两**岸**，于是在岸边总有**船夫**等待要**渡江**的人们。

gǔ dài de zhōng guó **fèn chéng** hěn duō gè xiǎo guó jiā, **qí zhōng** yǒu yī gè guó jiā jiào **chǔ guó**. zài chǔ guó de yī chù yǒu yī tiáo **jiāng,** jiāng miàn kuān kuò, jiāng shuǐ tuān jí, bì xū **chéng chuán** cái néng **wǎng fǎn** yú jiāng de liǎng **àn,** yú shì zài àn biān zǒng yǒu **chuán fū** děng dài yào **dù jiāng** de rén men.

这一天，江边来了一个男人。他个子很高，身材壮实，**腰间**还挂着一把长**剑**和一把**匕首**。在那时候的楚国，男人们**佩**剑是很常见的事情。他走到一艘**渡船**边停下来，船夫便走上前来问道："先生，请问您是要渡江吗？"男人回答道："是的。"船夫便让他上了船。小木船非常简单，两侧**船舷**之间有一个小小的**船舱**。**乘客**见船舱又小又**窄**，便坐在了外面的**甲板**上。他把长剑从腰间取下，放在旁边。船夫用一根长长的**竹竿**在岸上一**撑**，小船就离开了岸边。

zhè yī tiān, jiāng biān lái le yī gè nán rén. tā gè zǐ hěn gāo, shēn cái zhuàng shí, **yāo jiān** hái guà zhe yī bǎ cháng **jiàn** hé yī bǎ **bǐ shǒu**. zài nà shí hòu de chǔ guó, nán rén men **pèi** jiàn shì hěn cháng jiàn de shì qíng. tā zǒu dào yī sōu **dù chuán** biān tíng xià lái, chuán fū biàn zǒu shàng qián lái wèn dào: "xiān shēng, qǐng wèn nín shì yào dù jiāng ma?" nán rén huí dá dào: "shì de." chuán fū biàn ràng tā shàng le chuán. xiǎo mù chuán fēi cháng jiǎn dān, liǎng cè **chuán xián** zhī jiān yǒu yī gè xiǎo xiǎo de **chuán cāng**. **chéng kè** jiàn chuán cāng yòu xiǎo yòu **zhǎi**, biàn zuò zài le wài miàn de **jiǎ bǎn** shàng. tā bǎ zhǎng jiàn cóng yāo jiān qǔ xià, fàng zài páng biān. chuán fū yòng yī gēn cháng cháng de **zhú gān** zài àn shàng yī **chēng**, xiǎo chuán jiù lí kāi le àn biān.

船夫**熟练**地撑着船在水中前进，他经常会跟坐船的人**闲谈**，于是对男人说："先生，您是从哪里来的呀？"男人回答："从那边的村庄里来，要到城里去。"船夫**点点头**说："城里可热闹了，**商铺**里好多**新鲜玩意儿**。"男人**摆摆手**道："你们这些乡下人才觉得那些是新鲜玩意儿，我**走南闯北**，见得多了，在我眼里那些都不算什么。"船夫笑着问道："看来先生是**见多识广**了，不知道您是做什么的呢？"男人拍拍**胸膛**，说："我是个**剑客**，**官府**会请我去帮忙**捉拿罪犯**，**尊贵的**官员和**有钱人**家里也会请我去保护他们的安全和财产。我**不光**去过楚国的很多地方，**还到**过别的国家。"船夫**佩服**地说："啊，那您的**剑术**一定非常**高明**了。"剑客**骄傲**地说："那是当然，我让你**见识**见识。"他拿起身旁的长剑，站起身。船夫连忙说："这样太**危险**了，请您坐下。"可是剑客就像没听见一样，用剑在空中**挥舞**了起来。小船随之**摇晃**，剑客站立不稳，身体一歪，**不由自主**地松了手，长剑掉进了水里。

chuán fū **shú liàn** dì chēng zhe chuán zài shuǐ zhōng qián jìn, tā jīng cháng huì gēn zuò chuán de rén **xián tán**, yú shì duì nán rén shuō: "xiān shēng, nín shì cóng nǎ lǐ lái de ya?" nán rén huí dá: "cóng nà biān de cūn zhuāng lǐ lái, yào dào chéng lǐ qù." chuán fū **diǎn diǎn tóu** shuō: "chéng lǐ kě rè nào le, **shāng pù** lǐ hǎo duō **xīn xiān wán** yì ér. "nán rén **bǎi bǎi shǒu** dào: "nǐ men zhè xiē **xiāng xià rén** cái jué dé nà xiē shì xīn xiān wán yì ér, wǒ **zǒu nán chuǎng běi**, jiàn dé duō le, zài wǒ yǎn lǐ nà xiē dōu bú suàn shí me. "chuán fū xiào zhe wèn dào: "kàn lái xiān shēng shì **jiàn duō shí guǎng** le, bú zhī dào nín shì zuò shén me de ne? "nán rén pāi pāi **xiōng táng**, shuō: "wǒ shì gè **jiàn kè**, **guān fǔ** huì qǐng wǒ qù bāng máng **zhuō ná zuì fàn**, **zūn guì de** guān yuán hé **yǒu qián rén** jiā lǐ yě huì qǐng wǒ qù bǎo hù tā men de ān quán hé cái chǎn. wǒ **bú guāng** qù guò chǔ guó de hěn duō dì fāng, **hái** dào guò bié de guó jiā. "chuán fū **pèi fú** dì shuō: "ā, nà nín de **jiàn shù** yī dìng fēi cháng **gāo míng** le. "jiàn kè **jiāo ào** dì shuō: "nà shì dāng rán, wǒ ràng nǐ **jiàn shí** jiàn shí. "tā ná qǐ shēn páng de cháng jiàn, zhàn qǐ shēn. chuán fū lián máng shuō: "zhè yàng tài **wēi xiǎn** le, qǐng nín zuò xià. "kě shì jiàn kè jiù xiàng méi tīng jiàn yī yàng, yòng jiàn zài kōng zhōng **huī wǔ** le qǐ lái. xiǎo chuán suí zhī **yáo huàng**, jiàn kè zhàn lì bú wěn, shēn tǐ yī **wāi, bú yóu zì zhǔ** dì **sōng** le **shǒu**, cháng jiàn diào jìn le shuǐ lǐ.

船夫慌了，说："这下**糟了**！"但男人却**不慌不忙**地说："没关系，你只管继续**划船**，我自有办法。"船夫**将信将疑**，但只能**照办**。只见乘客**拔**出匕首，**对准**长剑落水的地方在船舷上**刻**了一道。船夫问："您这是在干什么？"剑客**得意**地说："我在此做个**记号**，这样到了对岸，就能把剑找回来了。你要知道，我不光剑术高明，而且见多识广，脑子也很聪明。"船夫感到十分困惑，但他不敢多问。

chuán fū huāng le, shuō: "zhè xià **zāo le**! "dàn nán rén què **bú huāng bú máng** dì shuō: "méi guān xì, nǐ zhī guǎn jì xù **huá chuán**, wǒ zì yǒu bàn fǎ. "chuán fū **jiāng xìn jiāng yí**, dàn zhī néng **zhào bàn**. zhī jiàn chéng kè **bá** chū bǐ shǒu, **duì zhǔn** cháng jiàn luò shuǐ de dì fāng zài chuán xián shàng **kè** le yī dào. chuán fū wèn: "nín zhè shì zài gàn shí me? "jiàn kè **dé yì** dì shuō: "wǒ zài cǐ zuò gè **jì hào**, zhè yàng dào le duì àn, jiù néng bǎ jiàn zhǎo huí lái le. nǐ yào zhī dào, wǒ bú guāng jiàn shù gāo míng, ér qiě jiàn duō shí guǎng, nǎo zǐ yě hěn cōng míng. "chuán fū gǎn dào shí fèn kùn huò, dàn tā bú gǎn duō wèn.

不一会儿，船靠岸了。乘客对船夫说："看我的！"他脱下衣服，看准做记号的地方一头跳进江水里。他绕着小船游来游去，潜入水中好几次，但什么也没有找到，无奈之下，只好爬上岸。他浑身湿漉漉，垂头丧气地问船夫："我明明做了记号，可为什么找不到我的剑呢？"船夫大笑道："聪明的剑客先生，记号虽然还在，但这里已经不是您长剑落水的地方了啊！"

bú yī huì ér, chuán **kào àn** le. chéng kè duì chuán fū shuō: "kàn wǒ de!"tā **tuō** xià **yī fú**, kàn zhǔn zuò jì hào de dì fāng yī tóu tiào jìn jiāng shuǐ lǐ. tā rào zhe xiǎo chuán yóu lái yóu qù, **qián** rù shuǐ zhōng hǎo jǐ cì, dàn shí me yě méi yǒu zhǎo dào, wú nài zhī xià, zhī hǎo pá shàng àn. tā **hún shēn shī lù lù**, **chuí tóu sàng qì** dì wèn chuán fū: "wǒ **míng míng** zuò le jì hào, kě wéi shí me zhǎo bú dào wǒ de jiàn ne?"chuán fū dà xiào dào: "cōng míng de jiàn kè xiān shēng, jì hào suī rán hái zài, dàn zhè lǐ yǐ jīng bú shì nín cháng jiàn luò shuǐ de dì fāng le ā!"

总结 （zǒng jié- Summary

在古代的楚国，一位自以为见多识广而聪明能干的剑客乘船渡江。途中，他对船夫吹嘘自己的剑术，长剑不慎落入了水中。他便在船舷上做记号，登船靠岸了再按照记号跳下水去寻找长剑。这就是"刻舟求剑"这个成语的来历。

zài gǔ dài de chǔ guó, yī wèi zì yǐ wéi jiàn duō shí guǎng ér cōng míng néng gàn de jiàn kè chéng chuán dù jiāng. tú zhōng, tā duì chuán fū chuī xū zì jǐ de jiàn shù, cháng jiàn bú shèn luò rù le shuǐ zhōng. tā biàn zài chuán xián shàng zuò jì hào, dēng chuán kào àn le zài àn zhào jì hào tiào xià shuǐ qù xún zhǎo cháng jiàn. zhè jiù shì"kè zhōu qiú jiàn "zhè gè chéng yǔ de lái lì.

Summary of the story

In the Chu State of ancient China, a swordsman who thinks highly of himself takes a ferry boat to cross a river. On the boat, he boasts about his knowledge and experience to the boatman, and tries to show off his swordsmanship, which then causes him to drop his sword into the river. He carves a mark on the ship board. When the boat arrives on the other side of the river, he jumps into the water, hoping to find his sword following the mark. But he simply doesn't understand that the boat has moved.

Vocabulary

- **分成 (fèn chéng):** be divided into
- **其中 (qí zhōng):** among those
- **楚国 (chǔ guó):** the State of Chu
- **江 (jiāng):** river
- **乘船 (chéng chuán):** to travel by boat/ship
- **往返 (wǎng fǎn):** back and forth
- **岸 (àn):** bank, shore
- **船夫 (chuán fū):** boatman
- **渡江 (dù jiāng):** to cross a river
- **腰间 (yāo jiān):** around one's waist
- **剑 (jiàn):** sword
- **匕首 (bǐ shǒu):** dagger
- **佩 (pèi):** to wear (as adornments)
- **渡船 (dù chuán):** ferry, ferryboat

- **船舷 (chuán xián):** side of a ship/boat, ship board
- **船舱 (chuán cāng):** cabin, compartment of a ship/boat
- **乘客 (chéng kè):** passenger
- **窄 (zhǎi):** narrow
- **甲板 (jiǎ bǎn):** deck
- **竹竿 (zhú gān):** bamboo pole
- **撑 (chēng):** to push or move with a pole
- **熟练 (shú liàn):** skilled, proficient
- **闲谈 (xián tán):** to have a casual chat
- **点点头 (diǎn diǎn tóu):** to nod
- **商铺 (shāng pù):** store
- **新鲜 (xīn xiān):** fresh, new
- **玩意儿 (wán yì ér):** thing, plaything

- 摆摆手 (bǎi bǎi shǒu): to wave one's hand (to reject)
- 乡下人 (xiāng xià rén): chuff, peasant
- 走南闯北 (zǒu nán chuǎng běi): to travel extensively
- 见多识广 (jiàn duō shí guǎng): to have a wide range of experience and knowledge
- 胸膛 (xiōng táng): chest
- 剑客 (jiàn kè): swordsman
- 官府 (guān fǔ): the (local) ruling authorities
- 捉拿 (zhuō ná): to catch, to arrest
- 罪犯 (zuì fàn): a criminal
- 尊贵的 (zūn guì de): prestigious, honorable
- 有钱人 (yǒu qián rén): rich people
- 不光……还 (bú guāng……hái): not only...but also
- 佩服 (pèi fú): to admire
- 剑术 (jiàn shù): swordsmanship
- 高明 (gāo míng): brilliant
- 骄傲 (jiāo ào): proud, conceited
- 见识 (jiàn shí): to see, to gain experience
- 危险 (wēi xiǎn): dangerous
- 挥舞 (huī wǔ): to wield, to wave
- 摇晃 (yáo huàng): to sway, to rock
- 歪 (wāi): not straight, deflected
- 不由自主 (bú yóu zì zhǔ): involuntarily, beyond one's control
- 松手 (sōng shǒu): to loosen one's grip, to let go
- 糟了 (zāo le): this is terrible, too bad
- 不慌不忙 (bú huāng bú máng): not in a hurry or panic

99

- 划船 (huá chuán): row or paddle a boat
- 将信将疑 (jiāng xìn jiāng yí): half believing, half doubting
- 照办 (zhào bàn): to act accordingly, comply with
- 拔 (bá): to pull
- 对准 (duì zhǔn): to aim at
- 刻 (kè): to carve, to cut
- 得意 (dé yì): complacent, be proud of oneself
- 记号 (jì hào): mark
- 不一会儿 (bú yī huì ér): before long, soon, in a while
- 靠岸 (kào àn): to pull in to shore
- 脱衣服 (tuō yī fú): to take off clothes
- 潜 (qián): to dive
- 浑身 (hún shēn): all over the body
- 湿漉漉 (shī lù lù): wet
- 垂头丧气 (chuí tóu sàng qì): be in low spirits
- 明明 (míng míng): obviously, undoubtedly

Questions about the story

1. 故事中的江两岸分别是？

   gù shì zhōng de jiāng liǎng àn fēn bié shì?

   a) 村庄和城市

   cūn zhuāng hé chéng shì

   b) 楚国和别的国家

   chǔ guó hé bié de guó jiā

   c) 两个城市

   liǎng gè chéng shì

2. 根据故事中的内容，剑客的工作不包括以下哪一项：

   gēn jù gùshì zhōng de nèiróng, jiàn kè de gōngzuò bù bāo kuò

   yǐ xià nǎ yī xiàng:

   a) 捉拿罪犯

   zhuō ná zuì fàn

   b) 保护有钱人的财产

   bǎo hù yǒu qián rén de cái chǎn

   c) 在城市里巡逻

   zài chéng shì lǐ xún luó

3. 乘客的剑是怎么掉进水里的？

   chéng kè de jiàn shì zěn me diào jìn shuǐ lǐ de?

   a) 因为风浪太大

   yīn wèi fēng làng tài dà

   b) 因为船夫要看他的剑术

   yīn wèi chuán fū yào kàn tā de jiàn shù

c) 因为他想要船夫见识他的剑术

yīn wèi tā xiǎng yào chuán fū jiàn shì tā de jiàn shù

4. 乘客为什么要在船舷上刻记号？

chéng kè wéi shén me yào zài chuán xián shàng kè jì hào?

a) 为了纪念失去了自己的剑

wèi le jì niàn shī qù le zìjǐ de jiàn

b) 因为他认为这样可以把剑找回来

yīn wèi tā rèn wéi zhè yàng kě yǐ bǎ jiàn zhǎo huí lái

c) 因为他很生气

yīn wèi tā hěn sheng qì

5. 从这个故事里可以推断，刻舟求剑这个成语形容的是：

cóng zhè ge gù shì lǐ kě yǐ tuī duàn, kè zhōu qiú jiàn zhè ge chéng yǔ xíng róng de shì:

a) 不懂得灵活变通的人

bù dǒng dé líng huó biàn tōng de rén

b) 聪明的人

cōng míng de rén

c) 见多识广的人

jiàn duō shì guǎng de rén

Answers

1. A
2. C
3. C
4. B
5. A

Chapter X

毕业旅行 (BÌ YÈ LǓ XÍNG)

汉森是一名**德国大学生**，他**主修计算机工程**，成绩优秀。因为非常喜欢中国文化，所以他**自学**了中文。汉森大学**毕业**前几个月，他的父母问："汉森，毕业以后你打算做什么呢，是找工作，还是继续**深造**？"汉森**不假思索**地说："我要先去旅行。我在大学里学习了很多**知识**，但是对学校外面的世界了解还太少。我要看一看外面的世界，然后决定自己的方向。"父母很支持他的想法。

hàn sēn shì yī míng **dé guó dà xué shēng**, tā **zhǔ xiū jì suàn jī gōng chéng**, chéng jì yōu xiù. yīn wéi fēi cháng xǐ huān zhōng guó wén huà, suǒyǐ tā **zì xué** le zhōng wén. hàn sēn dà xué **bì yè** qián jǐ gè yuè, tā de fù mǔ wèn: "hàn sēn, bì yè yǐ hòu nǐ dǎ suàn zuò shí me ne, shì zhǎo gōng zuò, hái shì jì xù **shēn zào**? "hàn sēn **bú jiǎ sī suǒ** dì shuō: "wǒ yào xiān qù lǚ xíng. wǒ zài dà xué lǐ xué xí le hěn duō **zhī shí**, dàn shì duì xué xiào wài miàn de shì jiè liǎo jiě hái tài shǎo. wǒ yào kàn yī kàn wài miàn de shì jiè, rán hòu jué dìng zì jǐ de fāng xiàng. "fù mǔ hěn zhī chí tā de xiǎng fǎ.

汉森对于这件事早就有计划，旅行的**目的地**也想好了：中国。他一直向往能自己去到中国，看一看那些书上和电视里看到过的地方，**不仅如此**，他知道计算机和**互联网**在中国发展迅速，也许他能在那里**发现**惊喜呢！

hàn sēn duì yú zhè jiàn shì zǎo jiù yǒu jì huá, lǚ xíng de **mù de dì** yě xiǎng hǎo le: zhōng guó. tā yī zhí xiàng wǎng néng zì jǐ qù dào zhōng guó, kàn yī kàn nà xiē shū shàng hé diàn shì lǐ kàn dào guò de dì fāng, **bú jǐn rú cǐ**, tā zhī dào jì suàn jī hé **hù lián wǎng** zài zhōng guó fā zhǎn xùn sù, yě xǔ tā néng zài nà lǐ **fā xiàn** jīng xǐ ne!

六月，毕业**典**礼结束后的第二天，汉森就登上了去上海的飞机。经过近二十个小时，他到达**浦东机场**，开始了中国之旅。在一个月的时间里，他踏足许多地方：北京的**长城、故宫博物院**和**颐和园**，西安的**兵马俑**，杭州的**西湖**和**灵隐寺**，苏州的**园林**，安徽的**黄山**，江西的**庐山**。他还乘船游览了**长江三峡**。一路上，他也享受了各地的美食，从**北京烤鸭**到四川**火锅**，全都让他**念念不忘**。

liù yuè, bì yè **diǎn lǐ** jié shù hòu de dì èr tiān, hàn sēn jiù dēng shàng le qù shàng hǎi de fēi jī. jīng guò jìn èr shí gè xiǎo shí, tā dào dá **pǔ dōng jī chǎng**, kāi shǐ le zhōng guó zhī lǚ. zài yī gè yuè de shí jiān lǐ, tā tàzú xǔ duō dì fāng: běi jīng de **cháng chéng, gù gōng bó wù yuàn** hé **yí hé yuán**, xī ān de **bīng mǎ yǒng**, háng zhōu de **xī hú** hé **líng yǐn sì**, sū zhōu de **yuán lín**, ān huī de **huáng shān**, jiāng xī de **lú shān**. tā hái chéng chuán yóu lǎn le **cháng jiāng sān xiá**. yī lù shàng, tā yě xiǎng shòu le gè dì de měi shí, cóng **běi jīng kǎo yā** dào sì chuān **huǒ guō**, quán dōu ràng tā **niàn niàn bú wàng**.

在所有地方中，他最喜欢的是上海。这是他到中国的**第一站**，也令他**印象**最深刻。上海是一个**国际化**的大**都市**，有着无数的**高楼大厦**，街上有川流不息的人和车，地铁**四通八达**。**外滩**有漂亮的建筑，尤其是**黄浦江**上的**夜景**格外迷人。这里也是中国的**金融**和**科技中心**，有来自世界各地的**企业**，许多人能说英语，汉森也看到了不少外国人。他不由得想，如果能在这里工作生活该有多好啊。

zài suǒ yǒu dì fāng zhōng, tā zuì xǐ huān de shì shàng hǎi. zhè shì tā dào zhōng guó de **dì yī zhàn**, yě lìng tā **yìn xiàng** zuì **shēn kè**. shàng hǎi shì yī gè **guó jì huà** de dà **dū shì**, yǒu zhe **wú shù** de **gāo lóu dà shà**, jiē shàng yǒu chuān liú bú xī de rén hé chē, dì tiě **sì tōng bā dá**. **wài tān** yǒu piāo liàng de jiàn zhù, yóu qí shì **huáng pǔ jiāng** shàng de **yè jǐng** gé wài mí rén. zhè lǐ yě shì zhōng guó de **jīn róng** hé **kē jì zhōng xīn**, yǒu lái zì shì jiè gè dì de **qǐ yè**, xǔ duō rén néng shuō yīng yǔ, hàn sēn yě kàn dào le bú shǎo wài guó rén. tā bú yóu dé xiǎng, rú guǒ néng zài zhè lǐ gōng zuò shēng huó gāi yǒu duō hǎo ā.

旅行即将结束，汉森回到上海准备坐飞机返回德国。**临行前**的一天，他来到一家**跨国快递**公司，打算把自己旅途中购买的**纪念品**用**包裹寄**回家。走进**接待厅**，却有很多人**排队**，一位**女接待员**走过来对他用英语说："先生，**很抱歉**，我们的**内部网络系统**出了**故障**，影响服务，需要等待。"汉森用中文回答："没关系，请问要等多久呢？"对方说："您的中文说得真不错！**维修人员**还要两个小时才能到。"汉森微笑道："谢谢**夸奖**。我是学计算机的，或许我能帮得上忙？"

lǚ háng jí jiāng jié shù, hàn sēn huí dào shàng hǎi zhǔn bèi zuò fēi jī fǎn huí dé guó. **lín xíng** qián de yī tiān, tā lái dào yī jiā **kuà guó kuài dì** gōng sī, dǎ suàn bǎ zì jǐ lǚ tú zhōng gòu mǎi de **jì niàn pǐn** yòng **bāo guǒ jì** huí jiā. zǒu jìn **jiē dài tīng**, què yǒu hěn duō rén **pái duì**, yī wèi nǚ **jiē dài yuán** zǒu guò lái duì tā yòng yīng yǔ shuō: "xiān shēng, **hěn bào qiàn**, wǒ men de **nèi bù wǎng luò xì tǒng** chū le **gù zhàng**, yǐng xiǎng fú wù, xū yào děng dài. "hàn sēn yòng zhōng wén huí dá: "méi guān xì, qǐng wèn yào děng duō jiǔ ne?"duì fāng shuō: "nín de zhōng wén shuō dé zhēn bú cuò! **wéi xiū rén yuán** hái yào liǎng gè xiǎo shí cái néng dào. "hàn sēn wēi xiào dào: "xiè xiè **kuā jiǎng**. wǒ shì xué jì suàn jī de, huò xǔ wǒ néng bāng dé shàng máng?"

第二天，汉森的包裹**启程**去德国了，里面除了**礼物**和纪念品，还有一封给父母的**信**：

dì èr tiān, hàn sēn de bāo guǒ **qǐ chéng** qù dé guó le, lǐ miàn chú le **lǐ wù** hé jì niàn pǐn, hái yǒu yī fēng gěi fù mǔ de **xìn**：

爸爸、妈妈：

bà bà, mā mā：

你们一定想不到，我要留在中国工作了！我帮助这里的一家快递公司**解决**了他们的电脑网络故障。公司经理**认可**我的能力，并且发现我能说**德语**、中文和英语，对他们的工作很有帮助，于是决定**聘用**我。我将会留在上海。

nǐ men yī dìng xiǎng bú dào, wǒ yào liú zài zhōng guó gōng zuò le! wǒ bāng zhù zhè lǐ de yī jiā kuài dì gōng sī **jiě jué** le tā men de diàn nǎo wǎng luò gù zhàng. gōng sī jīng lǐ **rèn kě** wǒ de néng lì, bìng qiě fā xiàn wǒ néng shuō **dé yǔ**, zhōng wén hé yīng yǔ, duì tā men de gōng zuò hěn yǒu bāng zhù, yú shì jué dìng **pìn yòng** wǒ. wǒ jiāng huì liú zài shàng hǎi.

圣诞节我会回家**探望**，请你们有时间的话也来中国看看吧，我相信你们会喜欢这里的！

shèng dàn jiē wǒ huì huí jiā **tàn wàng**, qǐng nǐ men yǒu shí jiān de huà yě lái zhōng guó kàn kàn ba, wǒ xiàng xìn nǐ men huì xǐ huān zhè lǐ de!

爱你们的
汉森

ài nǐ men de
hàn sēn

总结 （zǒng jié- Summary

德国青年汉森大学毕业后去中国旅行，想借此了解情况，对自己未来的方向做判断。他游览了中国的许多地方，尤其喜欢上海。就在他离开中国的前一天，凭借自己的专业能力和语言优势，他获得了留在上海工作的机会。

dé guó qīng nián hàn sēn dà xué bì yè hòu qù zhōng guó lǚ xíng, xiǎng jiè cǐ liǎo jiě qíng kuàng, duì zì jǐ wèi lái de fāng xiàng zuò pàn duàn. tā yóu lǎn le zhōng guó de xǔ duō dì fāng, yóu qí xǐ huān shàng hǎi. jiù zài tā lí kāi zhōng guó de qián yī tiān, píng jiè zì jǐ de zhuān yè néng lì hé yǔ yán yōu shì, tā huò dé le liú zài shàng hǎi gōng zuò de jī huì.

Summary of the story

Hansen, a young man from Germany, decides to make a trip to China after graduating from college. He wants to see what it's like there to make a decision about his future. He travels around China and sees many famous places. Among those place, his favourite is Shanghai. The day before leaving China for Germany, Hansen has got a job offer due to his skills in computer technology and language. He is very happy to be able to stay in Shanghai .

Vocabulary

- 德国 (**dé guó**): Germany
- 大学生 (**dà xué shēng**): college student, undergraduate
- 主修 (**zhǔ xiū**): major, to specialize in
- 计算机工程 (**jì suàn jī gōng chéng**): computer engineering
- 自学 (**zì xué**): to teach oneself, to learn by oneself
- 毕业 (**bì yè**): to graduate
- 深造 (**shēn zào**): to pursue further education
- 不假思索 (**bú jiǎ sī suǒ**): without thinking
- 知识 (**zhī shí**): knowledge
- 目的地 (**mù de dì**): destination
- 不仅如此 (**bú jǐn rú cǐ**): not only, in addition
- 互联网 (**hù lián wǎng**): the Internet
- 发现 (**fā xiàn**): discoveries
- 典礼 (**diǎn lǐ**): ceremony
- 浦东机场 (**pǔ dōng jī chǎng**): Pudong International Airport
- 长城 (**cháng chéng**): The Great Wall
- 故宫博物院 (**gù gōng bó wù yuàn**): The Palace Museum
- 颐和园 (**yí hé yuán**): The Summer Palace
- 兵马俑 (**bīng mǎ yǒng**): The Terracota Army
- 西湖 (**xī hú**): The West Lake
- 灵隐寺 (**líng yǐn sì**): the Lingyin Temple
- 园林 (**yuán lín**): Chinese landscaped garden
- 黄山 (**huáng shān**): the Huangshan Mountain
- 庐山 (**lú shān**): Mount Lu

- 长江三峡 (cháng jiāng sān xiá): The Three Gorges along the Yangtze River
- 北京烤鸭 (běi jīng kǎo yā): Peking roast duck
- 火锅 (huǒ guō): hot pot
- 念念不忘 (niàn niàn bú wàng): to think constantly of, to be always in mind
- 第一站 (dì yī zhàn): the first stop
- 印象深刻 (yìn xiàng shēn kè): be deeply impressed
- 国际化 (guó jì huà): international
- 都市 (dū shì): metropolis, city
- 无数 (wú shù): countless, numerous
- 高楼大厦 (gāo lóu dà shà): high-rise buildings
- 四通八达 (sì tōng bā dá): be accessible from all directions
- 外滩 (wài tān): The Bund
- 黄浦江 (huáng pǔ jiāng): the Huangpu River
- 夜景 (yè jǐng): night scene/view
- 金融 (jīn róng): finance
- 科技 (kē jì): science and technology
- 中心 (zhōng xīn): center, hub
- 企业 (qǐ yè): corporate, company
- 临行 (lín xíng): before departure
- 跨国 (kuà guó): cross-national
- 快递 (kuài dì): express delivery
- 纪念品 (jì niàn pǐn): souvenir
- 包裹 (bāo guǒ): package
- 寄 (jì): to send by post
- 接待厅 (jiē dài tīng): reception lobby
- 排队 (pái duì): to queue, to line in a queue

- **接待员 (jiē dài yuán):** receptionist
- **很抱歉 (hěn bào qiàn):** (we are) very sorry
- **内部 (nèi bù):** internal
- **网络 (wǎng luò):** network
- **系统 (xì tǒng):** system
- **故障 (gù zhàng):** malfunction
- **维修人员 (wéi xiū rén yuán):** maintenance technician
- **夸奖 (kuā jiǎng):** praise

- **启程 (qǐ chéng):** to set out on a journey
- **礼物 (lǐ wù):** gift, present
- **信 (xìn):** letter
- **解决 (jiě jué):** to solve a problem
- **认可 (rèn kě):** to recognize, to acknowledge
- **德语 (dé yǔ):** the German language
- **聘用 (pìn yòng):** to hire
- **圣诞节 (shèng dàn jiē):** Christmas
- **探望 (tàn wàng):** to visit

Questions about the story

1. 汉森在大学里主修什么专业？

   hàn sēn zài dà xué lǐ zhǔ xiū shén me zhuān yè?

   a) 中文

   zhōng wén

   b) 计算机工程

   jì suàn jī gōng chéng

   c) 旅游

   lǚ yóu

2. 汉森大学毕业后的计划是什么？

   hàn sēn dà xué bì yè hòu de jì huà shì shén me?

   a) 找工作

   zhǎo gōng zuò

   b) 继续深造

   jì xù shēn zào

   c) 旅行增长见识

   lǚ xíng zēng zhǎng jiàn shì

3. 下面哪一个地方是文中没有提到汉森曾去过的？

   xià miàn nǎ yī gè dì fāng shì wén zhōng méi yǒu tí dào hàn sēn céng qù guò de?

   a) 北京

   běi jīng

   b) 广州

   guǎng zhōu

c) 上海

shàng hǎi

4. 汉森喜欢上海的理由中不包括？

hàn sēn xǐ huān shàng hǎi de lǐ yóu zhōng bù bāo kuò?

   a) 上海非常国际化

   shàng hǎi fēi cháng guó jì huà

   b) 上海的物价比较高

   shàng hǎi de wù jià bǐ jiào gāo

   c) 外滩的风景很美

   wài tān de fēng jǐng hěn měi

5. 从汉森写给父母的信中可以推断：

cóng hàn sēn xiě gěi fù mǔ de xìn zhōng kě yǐ tuī duàn:

   a) 接待员同意了让汉森尝试修复故障

   jiē dài yuán tóng yì le ràng hàn sēn cháng shì xiū fù gù zhàng

   b) 汉森的父母不喜欢中国

   hàn sēn de fù mǔ bù xǐ huān zhōng guó

   c) 汉森的父母圣诞节会去中国

   hàn sēn de fù mǔ sheng dàn jié huì qù zhōng guó

Answers

1. B
2. C
3. B
4. B
5. A

CONCLUSION

Hello again, reader!

We hope you've enjoyed our stories and the way we've presented them. Each chapter, as you will have noticed, provides a way to practice vocabulary that you will use when speaking Chinese with the relevant background, while telling you something about the Chinese culture and ideology, as well as how people live and communicate nowadays in China.

Never forget: learning a language doesn't *have* to be a boring activity if you find the proper way to do it. Hopefully, we've provided you with a hands-on fun way to expand your knowledge in Chinese, and you can apply your lessons to future ventures.

Feel free to use this book in the future when you need to go back and review vocabulary and expressions — in fact, we encourage it.

If you have enjoyed this book and learned from it, please take a moment to leave a little review on the book, it's highly appreciated!

Believe in yourself and never be ashamed to make mistakes. Even the best can fall; it's those who get up that can achieve greatness! Take care!

MORE BOOKS BY LINGO MASTERY

Have you been trying to learn Chinese (Mandarin) and simply can't find the way to expand your vocabulary?

Do your teachers recommend you boring textbooks and complicated stories that you don't really understand?

Are you looking for a way to learn the language quicker without taking shortcuts?

If you answered *"Yes!"* to at least one of those previous questions, then this book is for you! We've compiled the **2000 Most Common Words in Chinese,** a list of terms that will expand your vocabulary to levels previously unseen.

Did you know that — according to an important study — learning the top two thousand (2000) most frequently used words will enable you to understand up to **84%** of all non-fiction and **86.1%**

of fiction literature and **92.7%** of oral speech? Those are *amazing* stats, and this book will take you even further than those numbers!

In this book:

- A detailed introduction with tips and tricks on how to improve your learning
- A list of **2000** of the most common words in Chinese and their translations
- An example sentence for each word – in both Chinese *and* English
- Finally, a conclusion to make sure you've learned and supply you with a final list of tips

Don't look any further, we've got what you need right here!

In fact, we're ready to turn you into a Chinese speaker... are you ready to become one?

So, you've decided to learn Chinese. Now what?

One of the toughest languages to learn, it's never been easy to find reading material in Chinese... However, we've created a book that will change all of that.

Language learning isn't just about lessons or practice – it's about *consistency*. You may have found the best teacher in town or the most incredible learning app around, but if you don't put all of that knowledge to practice, you'll soon forget everything you've obtained. This is why being engaged with interesting reading material can be so essential for somebody wishing to learn a new language.

Therefore, in this book we have compiled 20 easy-to-read, compelling and fun stories that will allow you to expand your vocabulary and give you the tools to improve your grasp of the wonderful Chinese (Mandarin) tongue.

How **Chinese Short Stories For Beginners** works:

- Each chapter possesses a funny, interesting and/or thought-provoking story based on real-life situations, allowing you to learn a bit more about the Chinese culture.

- Having trouble understanding Chinese characters? No problem – apart from the English translation below each paragraph, we've also provided you with the Pinyin romanization of the Chinese language, so that you never have trouble reading Chinese again!

- The summaries follow a synopsis in Chinese and in English of what you just read, both to review the lesson and for you to see if you understood what the tale was about. Use them if you're having trouble.

- At the end of those summaries, you'll be provided with a list of the most relevant vocabulary involved in the lesson, as well as slang and sayings that you may not have understood at first glance! Again, Pinyin romanization is included to make things super easy for you!

- Finally, you'll be provided with a set of tricky questions in Chinese, allowing you the chance to prove that you learned something in the story. Whether it's true or false, or if you're doing the single answer questions, don't worry if you don't know the answer to any — we will provide them immediately after, but no cheating!

We want you to feel comfortable while learning the tongue; after all, no language should be a barrier for you to travel around the world and expand your social circles!

So look no further! Pick up your copy of **Chinese Short Stories for Beginners** and level up your Chinese, *right now*!

Printed in Great Britain
by Amazon

86456257R00071